Frederic P. Miller, Agnes F. Vandome,
John McBrewster (Ed.)

Romanian Revolution of 1989

Frederic P. Miller, Agnes F. Vandome,
John McBrewster (Ed.)

Romanian Revolution of 1989

Romania, Communist Romania, Nicolae
Ceauşescu, History of Romania since 1989,
Revolutions of 1989, Braşov Rebellion, List
of books about the Romanian Revolution of
1989

Alphascript Publishing

Cover image: www.purestockx.com
Concerning the licence of the cover picture please contact PURESTOCKX.

Publisher: Alphascript Publishing is a trademark of VDM Publishing House Ltd.,17 Rue Meldrum, Beau Bassin,1713-01 Mauritius Email: info@vdm-publishing-house.com

Website: www.vdm-publishing-house.com

Published in 2009
Printed in: U.S.A., U.K., Germany. This book was not produced in Mauritius.

ISBN: 978-613-0-07956-7

Contents

Articles

References

Romanian Revolution of 1989

Romanian Revolution of 1989	
Part of the → Revolutions of 1989	
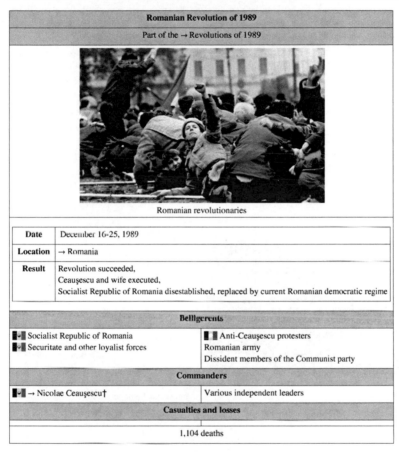 Romanian revolutionaries	
Date	December 16-25, 1989
Location	→ Romania
Result	Revolution succeeded, Ceaușescu and wife executed, Socialist Republic of Romania disestablished, replaced by current Romanian democratic regime
Belligerents	
Socialist Republic of Romania Securitate and other loyalist forces	Anti-Ceaușescu protesters Romanian army Dissident members of the Communist party
Commanders	
→ Nicolae Ceaușescu†	Various independent leaders
Casualties and losses	
1,104 deaths	

The **Romanian Revolution of 1989** was a week-long series of increasingly violent riots and fighting in late December 1989 that overthrew the Government of → Nicolae Ceaușescu. After a trial, Ceaușescu and his wife Elena were executed. → Romania was the only Eastern Bloc country to overthrow its government violently or to execute its leaders.

Background

Main article: → Communist Romania

See also: Nicolae Ceauşescu

As in neighboring countries, by 1989 the bulk of the Romanian population was dissatisfied with the Communist regime. However, unlike other Eastern Bloc countries, Romania had never undergone even limited de-Stalinization.Wikipedia:Citation needed Ceauşescu's economic and development policies (including grandiose construction projects such as the Palace of the Parliament and a draconian austerity program designed to enable Romania to liquidate its entire national debt in only a few years) were generally blamed for the country's painful shortages and widespread, increasing poverty. Parallel with increasing poverty, the secret police (*Securitate*) were becoming so ubiquitous as to make Romania essentially a police state.

Unlike the other Warsaw Pact leaders, Ceauşescu had not been slavishly pro-Soviet, but rather had pursued an "independent" foreign policy based on that of Josip Broz Tito's Yugoslavia. While Soviet leader Mikhail Gorbachev spoke of reform, Ceauşescu emulated the political hard-line, megalomania, and personality cults of East Asian communist leaders such as North Korea's Kim Il Sung. Even after the Berlin Wall fell and Ceauşescu's closest comrades, GDR's leader Eric Honecker resigned, and Bulgarian leader Todor Zhivkov was replaced in November 1989, Ceauşescu ignored the threat to his position as the last old-style communist leader in Eastern Europe.

Timişoara protest

Operei Square in Timişoara

On December 16, a protest broke out in Timişoara in response to an attempt by the government to evict a dissident, Hungarian Reformed pastor László Tőkés. Tőkés had recently made critical comments toward the regime in the Hungarian mediaWikipedia:Citation needed, and the government alleged that he was inciting ethnic hatred. At the behest of the government, his bishop removed him from his post, thereby depriving him of the right to use the apartment he was entitled to as a pastor, and sending him to be a pastor in countryside. For some time, his parishioners gathered around his home to protect him from harassment and eviction. Many passers-by, including religious Romanian students, spontaneously joined in.

History of Romania
This article is part of **a series**
Prehistory
Dacia
Dacian Wars
Roman Dacia
Thraco-Roman

Early Middle Ages
Origin of the Romanians
Middle Ages
History of Transylvania
Principality of Transylvania
Foundation of Wallachia
Foundation of Moldavia
Early Modern Times
Phanariotes
National awakening
Organic Statute
1848 Moldavian Revolution
1848 Wallachian Revolution
United Principalities
War of Independence
Kingdom of Romania
World War I
Greater Romania
World War II
Soviet occupation of Bessarabia and Northern Bukovina
→ **Communist Romania**
Soviet occupation
→ 1989 Revolution
→ **Romania since 1989**
Topic
Timeline
Military history
Romania Portal

As it became clear that the crowd would not disperse, the mayor, Petre Moţ, made remarks suggesting that he had overturned the decision to evict Tokes. Meanwhile, the crowd had grown impatient — and since Moţ declined to confirm his statement against the planned eviction in writing, the crowd started to chant anticommunist slogans. Consequently, police and *Securitate* forces showed up at the scene. By 7:30 p.m., the protest had spread out, and the original cause became largely irrelevant. Some of the protesters attempted to burn down the building that housed the District Committee of the Romanian Communist Party (PCR). The *Securitate* responded with tear gas and water jets, while the police beat up rioters and arrested many of them. Around 9:00 p.m., the rioters withdrew. They regrouped eventually around the Romanian Orthodox Cathedral and started a protest march around the city, but again they were confronted by the security forces.

Riots and protests resumed the following day, December 17. The rioters broke into the District Committee building and threw Party documents, propaganda brochures, Ceauşescu's writings, and other symbols of communist power out the windows. Again, the protesters attempted to set the building on fire, but this time they were stopped by military units. Since Romania did not have a riot police (Ceauşescu, who believed the Romanian people loved him, never saw the need for the formation of one), the military were sent in to control the riots, since the situation was too large for the *Securitate* and police to handle. The significance of the army presence in the streets was an ominous one: it meant that they had received their orders from the highest level of the command chain, presumably from Ceauşescu himself. The army failed to establish order and chaos ensued with gunfire, fights, casualties, and burned cars. Transport Auto Blindat (TAB) armored personnel carriers and tanks were called in. After 8:00 p.m., from Piaţa Libertăţii (Liberty Square) to the Opera there was wild shooting, including the area of Decebal bridge, Calea Lipovei (Lipovei Avenue), and Calea Girocului (Girocului Avenue). Tanks, trucks, and TABs blocked the accesses into the city while helicopters hovered overhead. After midnight the protests calmed down. Ion Coman, Ilie Matei, and Ştefan Guşă inspected the city, in which some areas looked like the aftermath of a war: destruction, ash, and blood.

The morning of December 18, the centre was being guarded by soldiers and *Securitate*-agents in plainclothes. Mayor Moţ ordered a Party gathering to take place at the University, with the purpose of condemning the "vandalism" of the previous days. He also declared martial law, prohibiting people from going about in groups larger than two people. Defying the curfew, a group of 30 young men headed for the Orthodox Cathedral, where they stopped and waved a Romanian flag from which they had removed the Romanian Communist coat of arms. Expecting that they would be fired upon, they started to sing "Deşteaptă-te, române!" (Wake up, Romanians), an earlier national song that had been banned since 1947. They were, indeed, fired upon and some died, and others were seriously injured, while the lucky ones were able to escape.

Operei Square in Timişoara

On December 19, Radu Bălan and Ştefan Guşă visited the workers in the city's factories, but failed to get them to resume work. On December 20, massive columns of workers were entering the city. About 100,000 protesters occupied Piaţa Operei (Opera Square — today Piaţa Victoriei, Victory Square) and started to chant anti-government protests: *"Noi suntem poporul!"* ("We are the people!"), *"Armata e cu noi!"* ("The army is on our side!"), *"Nu vă fie frică, Ceauşescu pică!"* ("Have no fear, Ceauşescu will fall"). Meanwhile, Emil Bobu and Constantin Dăscălescu were sent by Elena Ceauşescu (Nicolae Ceauşescu being at that time in Iran), to solve the situation. They met with a delegation of the protesters and accepted freeing the majority of the arrested protesters. However, they refused to comply with the protesters' main demand (resignation of Ceauşescu), and the situation remained essentially unchanged. The next day, trains loaded with workers originating from factories in Oltenia arrived in Timişoara. The regime was attempting to use them to repress the mass protests, but they finally ended up joining the protests. One worker explained: "Yesterday, our factory boss and a Party official rounded us up in the yard, handed us wood clubs and told us that Hungarians and 'hooligans' were devastating Timişoara and that it is our duty to go there and help crush the riots. But now I realize that this is not true."

On December 18, 1989, Ceauşescu had departed for a visit to Iran, leaving the duty of crushing the Timişoara revolt to his subordinates and his wife. Upon his return on the evening of December 20, the situation became even more tense, and he gave a televised speech from the TV studio inside the Central Committee Building (CC Building), in which he spoke about the events at Timişoara in terms of an "interference of foreign forces in Romania's internal affairs" and an "external aggression on Romania's sovereignty." The country, which had no information of the Timişoara events from the national media, heard about the Timişoara revolt from Western radio stations like Voice of America and Radio Free Europe, and by word of mouth. A mass meeting was staged for the next day, December 21, which, according to the official media, was presented as a "spontaneous movement of support for Ceauşescu," emulating the 1968 meeting in which Ceauşescu had spoken against the invasion of Czechoslovakia by the Warsaw

Pact forces.

The revolt spreads to Bucharest

Demonstrators on the street

On the morning of December 21, Ceauşescu addressed an assembly of approximately 110,000 people, to condemn the uprising in Timişoara. However, Ceauşescu was out of touch with his people and completely misread the crowd's mood. Starting his speech in the usual "wooden language, spurting out pro-socialist and Communist Party rhetoric," Ceauşescu delivered a litany of the achievements of the "socialist revolution" and Romanian "multi-laterally developed socialist society." The people, however, remained apathetic, and only the front rows supported Ceauşescu with cheers and applause. Ceauşescu's lack of understanding of the recent events and his incapacity to handle the situation were further demonstrated when he offered, as an act of desperation, to raise workers' salaries by 100 lei per month (about 4 US dollars at the time, yet a 5-10% raise for a modest salary) and student scholarship from 100 to 110 lei while continuing to praise the achievements of the Socialist Revolution, unable to realize that a revolution was brewing right in front of his eyes.

As he was addressing the crowd from the balcony of the Central Committee building, sudden movement came from the outskirts of the massed assembly, as did the sound of (what various sources have reported as) fireworks, bombs, or guns, which together caused the assembly to break into chaos. Initially frightened, the crowds tried to disperse. Bullhorns then began to spread the news that the Securitate was firing on the crowd and that a "revolution" was unfolding. This persuaded people in the assembly to join in. The rally turned into a protest demonstration.

The entire speech was being broadcast live around Romania, and it is estimated that perhaps 76% of the nation was watching. Censors attempted to cut the live video feed, and replace it with communist propaganda songs and video praising the Ceauşescu regime, but parts of the riots had already been broadcast and most of the Romanian people realized that something unusual was in progress.

Ceauşescu and his wife, as well as other officials and CPEx members, panicked, and Ceauşescu went into hiding inside the building.

The reaction of the Ceauşescu couple on the balcony is memorable: They staged futile attempts to regain control over the uprising crowd using phone conversation formulas such as *"Alo, Alo"* ("Hello, Hello"), Ceauşescu's wife "advised" him how to contain the situation *"Vorbeşte-le, vorbeşte-le"* ("Talk to them, talk to them"), and they urged the crowd *"Staţi liniştiţi la locurile voastre"* ("Stay quiet in your places"). In the end Ceauşescu allowed himself to be directed into the Central Committee building by his underlings.

The jeers and whistles soon erupted into riot; the crowd took to the streets, placing the capital, like Timişoara, in turmoil. Members of the crowd spontaneously began shouting anti-communist and anti-Ceauşescu slogans, which spread and became chants: *"Jos dictatorul!"* ("Down with the dictator"), *"Moarte criminalului!"* ("Death to the murderer"), *"Noi suntem poporul, jos cu dictatorul!"* ("We are the People, down with the dictator"), *"Ceauşescu cine eşti?/Criminal din Scorniceşti"* ("Ceauşescu, who are you? A murderer from Scorniceşti"). Protesters eventually flooded the downtown area, from Piaţa Kogălniceanu to Piaţa Unirii, Piaţa Rosetti, and Piaţa Romană. In one notable scene from the event, a young man waved a tricolour with the Communist coat of arms torn out of its center, while perched on the statue of Mihai Viteazul on Boulevard Mihail Kogălniceanu in the University Square.

As the hours passed, many more people took to the streets. Soon the protesters — unarmed and unorganized — were confronted by soldiers, tanks, TABs, USLA troops (*Unitatea Specială pentru Lupta Antiteroristă*, anti-terrorist special squads), and armed plain-clothes *Securitate* officers. The crowd was soon being shot at from various buildings, side streets, and tanks. There were many casualties, including deaths, as victims were shot, clubbed to death, stabbed, and crushed by armored vehicles (one TAB drove into the crowd around the InterContinental Hotel, crushing people — a French journalist, Jean Louis Calderon, was killed; a street near University Square was later named after him, as well as a high school in Timisoara). Firefighters hit the demonstrators with powerful water jets and the police continued to beat and arrest people. Protesters managed to build a defensible barricade in front of *Dunărea* ("Danube") restaurant, which stood until after midnight, but was finally torn apart by government forces. Intense continuous shooting continued until after 3:00 a.m., by which time the survivors had fled the streets.

Records of the fighting that day include footage shot from helicopters — sent to raid the area and to record evidence for eventual reprisals — as well as by tourists in the high tower of the centrally located InterContinental Hotel, next to the National Theater and across the street from the University.

It is likely that in the small hours of December 22, the Ceauşescus made their second mistake of the day: Instead of fleeing the city under cover of night, they decided to wait until morning to leave. Ceauşescu must have thought that his desperate attempts to crush the protests had succeeded, because he apparently called another meeting for the next morning. However, before 7:00 a.m., his wife Elena received the news that large columns of workers from many industrial platforms (large communist-era factories or groups of factories concentrated into industrial zones) were heading towards downtown Bucharest. The police barricades that were meant to block access to Piaţa Universităţii (University Square) and Piaţa Palatului (Palace Square, now Piaţa Revoluţiei — Revolution Square) proved useless. By 9:30 a.m., University Square was jammed with protesters. Security forces (army, police and others) re-entered the area, only to join with the protesters.

By 10 A.M., as the radio broadcast was announcing the introduction of martial law and of a ban on groups larger than five persons, yet hundreds of thousands of people were gathering for the first time, spontaneously, in central Bucharest (the previous day's crowd had come together at Ceauşescu's orders). Ceauşescu attempted to address the crowd from the balcony of the Central Committee of the Communist Party building, but his attempt was met with a wave of disapproval and anger. Helicopters spread manifestos (which did not reach the crowd, due to unfavourable winds) instructing people not to fall victim to the latest "diversion attempts," but to go home instead and enjoy the Christmas feast. This order, which drew unfavorable comparisons to Marie Antoinette's haughty "Let them eat cake", further infuriated the people, who at that time had trouble procuring such basic foodstuffs as cooking oil.

Ceauşescu falls

On the morning of December 22, sometime around 9:30 a.m., Vasile Milea, Ceauşescu's minister of defense, died under suspicious circumstances. A communique by Ceauşescu stated that Milea had been found to be a traitor and that he had committed suicide after his treason was revealed. The most widespread opinion at the time was that Milea had been assassinated because of his refusal to follow Ceauşescu's orders. In 2005 an investigation concluded that the minister killed himself by shooting at his heart, but the bullet missed the heart, hit an artery nearby, and he died soon afterwards.

Upon learning of Milea's apparent suicide, Ceauşescu appointed Victor Stănculescu as minister of defense. He accepted after a brief hesitation. Stănculescu, however, ordered the troops back to their quarters without Ceauşescu's knowledge, and moreover persuaded Ceauşescu to leave by helicopter, thus making the dictator a fugitive. By refusing to carry out the orders of Ceauşescu's (who was still technically commander-in-chief of the army), Stănculescu played a central role in the overthrow of the dictatorship. "I had the prospect of two execution squads: Ceauşescu's and the revolutionary one!" confessed Stănculescu later. In

Ceausescu's flight

the afternoon, Stănculescu "chose" Iliescu's political group from among others that were striving for power in the aftermath of the recent events.

At 11.20 on 22 December 1989, the commander of Ceauşescu's flight, Lieutenant-Colonel Vasile Malutan, received instructions from General Lieutenant Opruta to proceed to Palace Square to pick up the president. As he flew over Palace Square, he saw it was impossible to land there. Malutan landed his white Dauphin, no. 203, on the terrace at 11:44. A man brandishing a white net curtain from one of the windows waved him down. Malutan said, "Then Stelica, the co-pilot, came to me and said that there were demonstrators coming to the terrace. There the Ceauşescus came out, both practically carried by their bodyguards ... They look as if they were fainting. They were white with terror. Mănescu (one of the vice-presidents) and Bobu (Secretary to the Central Committee) were running behind them. Mănescu, Bobu, Neagoe and another Securitate officer scrambled to the four seats in the back ... As I pulled Ceauşescu in, I saw the demonstrators running across the terrace ... There wasn't enough space, Elena Ceauşescu and I were squeezed in between the chairs and the door .. We were only supposed to carry four passengers .. We had six." [1] According to Malutan, it was 12:08 when they left for Snagov. After they arrived there, Ceauşescu took Malutan into the presidential suite and ordered him to get two helicopters filled with soldiers for an armed guard, and a further Dauphin to come to Snagov. Malutan's unit commander replied on the phone, "There has been a revolution .. You are on your own ... Good luck!". Malutan then said to Ceauşescu that the second motor was now warmed up and they need to leave soon, but he could only take four people not six. Manescu and Bobu stayed behind. Ceauşescu then ordered Malutan to head for Titu. Near Titu, Malutan says that he made the helicopter dip up and down. He lied to Ceauşescu, saying that this was to avoid anti-aircraft fire, since they would now be in range. The dictator panicked and told him to land. [2]

He did so in a field next to the old road that led to Pitești. Malutan then told his four passengers that he could do nothing more. The Securitate men ran to the roadside and began to flag down passing cars. Two cars were flagged down, one of a forestry official and one a red Dacia of a local doctor. However, the local doctor was keen not to get involved and after a short time driving the Ceausescus faked engine trouble. A car of a bicycle repair man was then flagged down and he took them to Târgoviște. The driver of the car, Nicolae Petrișor, convinced them that they could hide successfully in an agricultural technical institute on the edge of town. When they arrived, the director guided the Ceausescus into a room and then locked them in. They were arrested by the local police at about 3:30 p.m., then after some wandering around transported to the Târgoviște garrison's military compound, and held captive for about 3 days, until their trial.[3] On 24 December, Ion Iliescu, head of the newly formed Council of the Front of National Salvation signed a Decree on the establishment of the Extraordinary Military Tribunal. The trial was held on December 25, lasted for about 2 hours, and delivered death-sentence for the couple. The execution followed immediately, on the spot, being carried out by three paratroopers with their service guns.

Footage of the trial and of the executed Ceaușescus was promptly released in Romania and to the rest of the world. The very moment of execution was not filmed since the cameraman was too slow, and he managed to get out into the court just as the shooting ended. [4]

The new regime

Dumitru Mazilu, Ion Iliescu and Petre Roman

After Ceaușescu left, the crowds in Palace Square entered a celebratory mood, perhaps even more intense than in the other former Eastern Bloc countries because of the recent violence. People cried, shouted, and gave each other gifts. The occupation of the Central Committee building continued. People threw Ceaușescu's writings, official portraits, and propaganda books out the windows, intending to burn them. They also promptly ripped off the giant letters from the roof making up the word *"comunist"* ("communist") in the slogan: "Trăiască Partidul Comunist Român!" ("Long live the Communist Party of Romania!"). A young woman appeared on the rooftop and waved a flag with the coat of arms torn or cut out.

At that time, fierce fights were underway at Bucharest Otopeni International Airport between troops sent one against another under claims that they were going to confront terrorists. According to a book by Ceaușescu's bodyguard, Securitate Lieutenant Colonel Dumitru Burlan, the generals who were part of the conspiracy led by General Stănculescu were trying to create fictional terrorism scenarios in order to induce fear and to push the army onto the side of the plotters.

However, the seizure of power by the new political structure National Salvation Front (FSN), which "emanated" from the second tier of the Communist Party leadership with help of the plotting generals, was not yet complete. Forces considered to be loyal to the old regime (spontaneously nicknamed "terrorists") opened fire on the crowd and attacked vital points of socio-political life: the television, radio, and telephone buildings, as well as Casa Scânteii (the center of the nation's print media, which serves a similar role today under the name Casa Presei Libere, "House of the Free Press") and the post office in the district of Drumul Taberei; Piaţa Palatului (site of the Central Committee building, but

Military and civilians fighting against Ceausescu's regime with the support of a BTR-60 armoured personnel carrier

also of the central university library, the national art museum, and the Ateneul Român, Bucharest's leading concert hall); the university and the adjoining Piaţa Universităţii (one of the city's main intersections); Otopeni and Băneasa airports; hospitals, and the Ministry of Defence.

During the night of December 22–December 23, Bucharest residents remained on the streets, especially in the attacked zones, fighting (and ultimately winning, even at the cost of many lives) a battle with an elusive and dangerous enemy. With the military confused by contradictory orders, true battles ensued, with many real casualties. At 9:00 p.m. on December 23, tanks and a few paramilitary units arrived to protect the Palace of the Republic.

Military fighting against the terrorist forces of the old regime (served with cakes by a civilian)

Meanwhile, messages of support were flooding in from all over the world: France (President François Mitterrand) ; the Soviet (President Mikhail Gorbachev); Hungary (the Hungarian Socialist Party); the new East German government (at that time the two German states were not yet formally reunited); Bulgaria (Petar Mladenov, General Secretary of the Communist Party of Bulgaria); Czechoslovakia (Ladislav Adamec, leader of the Communist Party of Czechoslovakia, and Vaclav Havel, the dissident writer, revolution leader and future president of the Republic); China (the Minister of Foreign Affairs); the United States (President George H. W. Bush) ; West Germany (Foreign Minister Hans Dietrich Genscher); NATO (Secretary General Manfred Wörner); the United Kingdom (Prime Minister Margaret Thatcher); Spain; Austria; the Netherlands; Italy; Portugal; Japan (the Japanese Communist Party); and the Moldavian SSR.

In the following days, moral support was followed by material support. Large quantities of food, medicine, clothing, medical equipment, etc., were sent to Romania. Around the world, the press dedicated entire pages and sometimes even complete issues to the Romanian revolution and its leaders.

On December 24, Bucharest was a city at war. Tanks, APCs, and trucks continued to go on patrol around the city and to surround trouble spots in order to protect them. At intersections near strategic objectives, roadblocks were built; automatic gunfire continued in and around Piaţa Universităţii, the Gara de Nord (the city's main railroad station), and

Piaţa Palatului. Yet amid the chaos, some people were seen to be clutching makeshift Christmas trees. "Terrorist activities" continued until December 27, when they abruptly stopped. Nobody ever found who conducted them, or who ordered their termination.

Casualties

The total number of deaths in the Romanian Revolution was 1,104, of which 162 were in the protests that led to the overthrow of → Nicolae Ceauşescu (December 16–22, 1989) and 942 in the fighting that occurred after the seizure of power by the new political structure National Salvation Front (FSN). The number of wounded was 3,352, of which 1,107 occurred while Ceauşescu was still in power and 2,245 after the National Salvation Front took power[5] [6].

Corpses lying in a morgue

Aftermath

Main article: → History of Romania since 1989

The Revolution brought Romania vast attention from the outside world. Initially, much of the world's sympathy inevitably went to the National Salvation Front government under Ion Iliescu, a former member of the Communist Party leadership and a Ceauşescu ally prior to falling into the dictator's disgrace in the early 1980s. The National Salvation Front, composed mainly of former members of the second echelon of the Communist Party, immediately assumed control over the state institutions, including the main media outlets, such as the national radio and television networks. They used their control of the media in order to launch virulent propaganda-style attacks against their new political opponents, the traditional democratic parties, which re-emerged after more than 50 years of underground activity.

"Empty" Romanian flags, from an exhibit at the Military Museum, Bucharest

Much of that sympathy was squandered during the Mineriad of January 1990 when miners and police, responding to Iliescu's appeals, invaded Bucharest and brutalized students and intellectuals who protested what they described as the hijacking of the Romanian Revolution by former members of the communist leadership under the auspices of the National Salvation Front, in an attempt to suppress any genuine political opposition.

In May 1990, partly due to the National Salvation Front's use of the media and of the partly preserved Communist Party infrastructure to silence the democratic opposition, Iliescu became Romania's first elected president after the revolution, with a majority of 85%. These elections have been condemned as undemocratic by both Romanian traditional parties and by the Western media.Wikipedia:Citation needed

Iliescu remained the central figure in Romanian politics for more than a decade, being re-elected for the third time in 2000, after a term out of power between 1996–2000. The survival of Ceauşescu's former ally demonstrated the ambiguity of the Romanian revolution, at once the most violent in 1989 and yet one that, according to some did not entirely replace the former regime.

Bibliography

- Ştefănescu, Domniţa *Cinci ani din Istoria României* ("Five years in the history of Romania"), 1995. Maşina de Scris, Bucharest.
- The series of 3 articles in the Romanian newspaper *Adevărul*, 2003 (see archives [7]) entitled "Eu am fost sosia lui Nicolae Ceauşescu" ("I was Ceauşescu's double"). These are about Col. Dumitru Burlan, who also wrote a book *Dupa 14 ani — Sosia lui Ceauşescu se destăinuie* ("After 14 Years — The Double of Ceauşescu confesses"). Editura Ergorom, July 31 2003. (All in Romanian.)
- Viorel Patrichi, "Eu am fost sosia lui Nicolae Ceauşescu [8]" ("I was Ceauşescu's double"), *Lumea Magazin* Nr 12, 2001 (in Romanian)
- Marian Oprea, "Au trecut 15 ani — Conspiraţia Securităţii" ("After 15 years — the conspiracy of Securitate"), *Lumea Magazin* Nr 10, 2004 [9]: (in Romanian; link leads to table of contents, verifying that the article exists, but the article itself is not online).
- Victor Stanculescu, "Nu vă fie milă, au 2 miliarde de lei în cont [10]" "Show no mercy, they have two billion lei [33 million U.S. dollars] in their bank account") in *Jurnalul Naţional*) Nov 22, 2004 (in Romanian)
- —, "Sinucidere - un termen acoperitor pentru crimă" [11] ("Suicide - a term to cover up a crime") in *Jurnalul Naţional* (retrieved from web site December 30 2004; no date indicated for original publication); on the death of Vasile Milea. (in Romanian)
- Nicolae Ceauşescu's speech [12], condemning the protests of Timişoara, broadcast on December 20 1989 (in Romanian)
- Mark Almond, *Uprising: Political Upheavals that have Shaped the World*, 2002. Mitchell Beazley, London.
- Marius Mioc, *Revoluţia din Timişoara* [13], *aşa cum a fost*, 1997, Brumar Publishing House, Timişoara (in Romanian)
- Marius Mioc, *The anticommunist Romanian Revolution* [14] *of 1989*, Marineasa Publishing House, Timişoara 2002
- Siani-Davies, Peter (2005 (2007)). *The Romanian Revolution of December 1989*. Ithaca, NY: Cornell University Press. ISBN 0-8014-4245-1, hardcover (ISBN 978-0-8014-7389-0, paperback).
- George Galloway and Bob Wylie, *Downfall: The Ceausescus and the Romanian Revolution*, 1991, Futura Publications, London. ISBN 0 7088 5003 0

See also

- → Revolutions of 1989
- → Braşov Rebellion
- → List of books about the Romanian Revolution of 1989
- → List of films about the Romanian Revolution of 1989

< → **Communist Romania** | **History of Romania** | → **Present Romania** >

External links

- Video of Nicolae Ceausescu's final speech [15] in Republican Square
- Anonymous Photo Essay about the Romanian Revolution of 1989 [16]
- TV broadcasts [17] from 22 and 23 of December 1989
- Video of Romanian Revolution of 1989 [18]

References

[1] George Galloway and Bob Wylie, *Downfall: The Ceausescus and the Romanian Revolution*, p. 168-169. Futura Publications, 1991

[2] George Galloway and Bob Wylie, *Downfall: The Ceausescus and the Romanian Revolution*, p. 170

[3] George Galloway and Bob Wylie, *Downfall: The Ceausescus and the Romanian Revolution*, p. 171

[4] George Galloway and Bob Wylie, *Downfall: The Ceausescus and the Romanian Revolution*, p. 199

[5] Revolution (http://timisoara.com/timisoara/revoluti.htm), Timisoara.

[6] Marius Mioc, *Revoluția din Timișoara așa cum fost*, 1997.

Romania

<table>
<tr><td colspan="2" align="center">Romania
România</td></tr>
<tr><td colspan="2"> </td></tr>
<tr><td colspan="2" align="center">Anthem: Deşteaptă-te, române!
Awaken, Romanian!</td></tr>
<tr><td colspan="2" align="center">

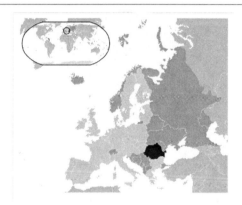

Location of → Romania(dark green)
— on the European continent(light green & dark grey)
— in the European Union(light green) — [Legend]
</td></tr>
<tr><td>Capital
(and largest city)</td><td>Bucharest (Bucureşti)
44°25′N 26°06′E44.417°N 26.1°E [1]</td></tr>
<tr><td align="center">Official languages</td><td>Romanian[1]</td></tr>
<tr><td>Ethnic groups</td><td>89.5% Romanians, 6.6% Hungarians, 2.5% Roma, 1.4% other minority groups</td></tr>
<tr><td align="center">Demonym</td><td>Romanian</td></tr>
<tr><td align="center">Government</td><td>Unitary semi-presidential republic</td></tr>
<tr><td>-</td><td>President</td><td>Traian Băsescu</td></tr>
<tr><td>-</td><td>Prime Minister</td><td>Emil Boc</td></tr>
<tr><td align="center" colspan="2">Legislature</td><td>Parliament</td></tr>
<tr><td>-</td><td>Upper House</td><td>Senate</td></tr>
<tr><td>-</td><td>Lower House</td><td>Chamber of Deputies</td></tr>
<tr><td align="center" colspan="2">Formation</td><td></td></tr>
<tr><td>-</td><td>Transylvania</td><td>10th century</td></tr>
</table>

-	Wallachia	1290
-	Moldavia	1346
-	First Unification	1599
-	Reunification of Wallachia and Moldavia	January 24, 1859
-	Officially recognised independence	July 13, 1878
-	Unification with Transylvania	December 1, 1918
EU accession		January 1, 2007
Area		
-	Total	238,391 km^2 (82nd) 92,043 sq mi
-	Water (%)	3
Population		
-	1 January 2009 estimate	21498616[1] (52nd)
-	2002 census	21,680,974
-	Density	90/km^2 (104th) 233/sq mi
GDP (PPP)		2008 estimate
-	Total	US$270.330 billion[2]
-	Per capita	US$12,579[2]
GDP (nominal)		2008 estimate
-	Total	US$199.673 billion[2]
-	Per capita	US$9,291[2]
Gini (2003)		31^2 (low) (21st)
HDI (2008)		▯ 0.825 (high) (62nd)
Currency		Leu (L)^2 (RON)
Time zone		EET (UTC+2)
-	Summer (DST)	EEST (UTC+3)
Drives on the		right
Internet TLD		.ro .eu
Calling code		40

[1] Other languages, such as Hungarian, German, Turkish, Crimean Tatar, Greek, Romani, Croatian, Ukrainian and Serbian, are official at various local levels.
[2] Romanian War of Independence.
[3] Treaty of Berlin.

Romania (pronounced /roʊˈmeɪniə/ (◀ listen); archaic: **Rumania, Roumania**; Romanian: *România* Romanian pronunciation: [romɨˈni.a] (◀ listen)) is a country located in Southeastern and Central Europe, North of the Balkan Peninsula, on the Lower Danube, within and outside the Carpathian arch, bordering on the Black Sea[3] . Almost all of the Danube Delta is located within its territory. It shares a border with Hungary and Serbia to the west, Ukraine and the Republic of Moldova to the northeast, and Bulgaria to the south.

The territory's recorded history includes periods of rule by Dacians, the Roman Empire, the Bulgarian empire, the Kingdom of Hungary, and the Ottoman Empire. As a nation-state, the country was formed by the merging of Moldavia and Wallachia in 1859 and it gained recognition of its independence in 1878. Later, in 1918, they were joined by Transylvania, Bukovina and Bessarabia. At the end of World War II, parts of its territories (roughly the present day Moldova) were occupied by the USSR and Romania became a member of the Warsaw Pact. With the fall of the Iron Curtain in → 1989, Romania started a series of political and economic reforms. After a decade of post-revolution economic problems, Romania made economic reforms such as low flat tax rates in 2005 and joined the European Union on January 1, 2007. While Romania's income level remains one of the lowest in the European Union, reforms have increased the growth speed. Romania is now an upper-middle income country economy.

Romania has the 9th largest territory and the 7th largest population (with 21.5 million people)[4] among the European Union member states. Its capital and largest city is Bucharest (Romanian: *Bucureşti* Romanian pronunciation: [buku'reʃtʲ] (◀ listen)), the 6th largest city in the EU with 1.9 million people. In 2007, Sibiu, a city in Transylvania, was chosen as a European Capital of Culture.[5] Romania also joined NATO on March 29, 2004, and is also a member of the Latin Union, of the Francophonie of the OSCE and an associate member of the CPLP. Romania is a semi-presidential unitary state.

Etymology

Main article: Etymology of Romania

The name of *Romania* (Romanian: *România*) comes from Romanian: *român* which is a derivative of the Latin: *Romanus* (Roman).[6] The fact that Romanians call themselves a derivative of *Romanus* (Romanian: *Român/Rumân*) is mentioned as early as the 16th century by many authors, including Italian Humanists travelling in Transylvania, Moldavia and Wallachia.[7] [8] [9] [10] The oldest surviving document written in the Romanian language is a 1521 letter known as "Neacşu's Letter from Câmpulung".[11] This document is also notable for having the first occurrence of "Rumanian" in a Romanian written text, Wallachia being here named The Rumanian Land – *Ţeara Rumânească* (*Ţeara* from the Latin: *Terra* land). In the following centuries, Romanian documents use interchangeably two spelling forms: *Român* and *Rumân*.[12] Socio-linguistic evolutions in the late 17th century led to a process of semantic differentiation: the form *"rumân"*, presumably usual among lower classes, got the meaning of "bondsman", while the form *român* kept an ethno-linguistic meaning.[13] After the abolition of serfdom in 1746, the form "rumân" gradually disappears and the spelling definitively stabilises to the form *"român"*, *"românesc"*.[14] The name "România" as common homeland of all Romanians is documented in the early 19th century.[15] This name has been officially in use since December 11, 1861.[16]

English-language sources still used the terms "Rumania" or "Roumania", borrowed from the French spelling *"Roumanie"*, as recently as World War II,[17] but since then those terms have largely been replaced with the official[18] spelling *"Romania"*.

History

Main article: History of Romania

Prehistory and Antiquity

Main articles: Prehistoric Balkans, Dacia, and Roman Dacia

The oldest modern human remains in Europe were discovered in the "Cave With Bones" in present day Romania.[19] The remains are approximately 42,000 years old and as Europe's oldest remains of *Homo sapiens*, they may represent the first such people to have entered the continent.[20] But the earliest written evidence of people living in the territory of the present-day Romania comes from Herodotus in book IV of his Histories (Herodotus) written 440 BCE, where he writes about the Getae tribes.[21]

A relief of Dacian king Decebalus from Trajan's Column

Dacians, considered a part of these Getae, were a branch of Thracians that inhabited Dacia (corresponding to modern Romania, Moldova and northern Bulgaria). The Dacian kingdom reached its maximum expansion during King Burebista, around 82 BC, and soon came under the scrutiny of the neighboring Roman Empire. After an attack by the Dacians on the Roman province of Moesia in 87 AD, the Romans led a series of wars (Dacian Wars) which eventually led to the victory of Emperor Trajan in 106 AD, and transformed the core of the kingdom into the province of Roman Dacia.[22]

Rich ore deposits were found in the province, and especially gold and silver were plentiful.[23] which led to Rome heavily colonizing the province.[24] This brought the Vulgar Latin and started a period of intense romanization, that would give birth to the proto-Romanian.[25] [26] Nevertheless, in the 3rd century AD, with the invasions of migratory populations such as Goths, the Roman Empire was forced to pull out of Dacia around 271 AD, thus making it the first province to be abandoned.[27] [28]

Several competing theories have been generated to explain the origin of modern Romanians. Linguistic and geo-historical analysis tend to indicate that Romanians have coalesced as a major ethnic group both South and North of the Danube.[29] *For further discussion, see Origin of Romanians.*

Middle Ages

Main articles: Romania in the Early Middle Ages and Romania in the Middle Ages

After the Roman army and administration left Dacia, the territory was invaded by the Goths,[30] then, in the 4th century by Huns.[31] They were followed by more nomads including Gepids,[32] [33] Avars,[34] Bulgars,[32] Pechenegs,[35] and Cumans.[36]

In the Middle Ages, Romanians lived in three distinct principalities: Wallachia (Romanian: *Ţara Românească*—"Romanian Land"), Moldavia (Romanian: *Moldova*) and Transylvania. By the 11th century, Transylvania became a largely autonomous part of the Kingdom of Hungary,[37] and became independent as the Principality of Transylvania from the 16th century,[38] until 1711.[39] In the other Romanian principalities, many small local states with

Bran Castle was built in 1212, and became commonly known as *Dracula's Castle* after the myths that it was the home of Vlad III the Impaler

varying degrees of independence developed, but only in the 14th century the larger principalities Wallachia (1310) and Moldavia (around 1352) emerged to fight a threat of the Ottoman Empire.[40] [41] Vlad III the Impaler maintained an independent policy in relation to the Ottoman Empire, and, in 1462, defeated Mehmed II's offensive during The Night Attack.[42]

By 1541, the entire Balkan peninsula and most of Hungary became Ottoman provinces. In contrast, Moldavia, Wallachia, and Transylvania, came under Ottoman suzerainty, but conserved fully internal autonomy and, until the 18th century, some external independence. During this period the Romanian lands were characterised by the slow disappearance of the feudal system; the distinguishment of some rulers like Stephen the Great, Vasile Lupu, and Dimitrie Cantemir in Moldavia, Matei Basarab, Vlad III the Impaler, and Constantin Brâncoveanu in Wallachia, Gabriel Bethlen in Transylvania; the Phanariot Epoch; and the appearance of the Russian Empire as a political and military influence.[43]

In 1600, the principalities of Wallachia, Moldova and Transylvania were simultaneously headed by the Wallachian prince Michael the Brave (*Mihai Viteazul*), Ban of Oltenia, but the chance for a unity dissolved after Mihai was killed, only one year later, by the soldiers of an Austrian army general Giorgio Basta. Mihai Viteazul, who was prince of Transylvania for less than one year, intended for the first time to unite the three principalities and to lay down foundations of a single state in a territory comparable to today's Romania.[44]

Moldavia, Wallachia and Transylvania at the end of the 16th century

After his death, as vassal tributary states, Moldova and Wallachia had complete internal autonomy and an external independence, which was finally lost in the 18th century. In 1699, Transylvania became a territory of the Habsburgs' Austrian empire, following the Austrian victory over the Turks in the Great Turkish War. The Austrians, in their turn, rapidly expanded their empire: in 1718 an important part of Wallachia, called Oltenia, was incorporated to the Austrian monarchy and was only returned in 1739. In 1775, the Austrian empire occupied the north-western part of Moldavia, later called Bukovina, while the eastern half of the principality (called Bessarabia) was occupied in

1812 by Russia.[43]

Independence and monarchy

Main articles: Early Modern Romania, National awakening of Romania, Romanian Principalities, Romanian War of Independence, and Kingdom of Romania

During the period of Austro-Hungarian rule in Transylvania, and Ottoman suzerainty over Wallachia and Moldavia, most Romanians were in the situation of being second-class citizens (or even non-citizens)[45] in a territory where they formed the majority of the population.[46] [47] In some Transylvanian cities, such as Braşov (at that time the Transylvanian Saxon citadel of Kronstadt), Romanians were not even allowed to reside within the city walls.[48]

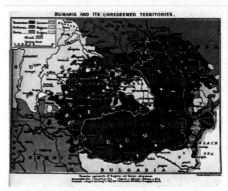

Territories inhabited by Romanians before WWI

After the failed 1848 Revolution, the Great Powers did not support the Romanians' expressed desire to officially unite in a single state, which forced Romania to proceed alone against the Ottomans. The electors in both Moldavia and Wallachia chose in 1859 the same person −Alexandru Ioan Cuza− as prince (*Domnitor* in Romanian).[49] Thus, Romania was created as a personal union, albeit a Romania that did not include Transylvania. There, the upper class and the aristocracy remained mainly Hungarian, and Romanian nationalism inevitably ran up against Hungarian in the late 19th century. As in the previous 900 years, Austria-Hungary, especially under the Dual Monarchy of 1867, kept the Hungarians firmly in control even in the parts of Transylvania where Romanians constituted a local majority.

In a 1866 *coup d'état*, Cuza was exiled and replaced by Prince Karl of Hohenzollern-Sigmaringen, who became known as Prince Carol of Romania. During the Russo-Turkish War Romania fought on the Russian side,[50] in and in the 1878 Treaty of Berlin, Romania was recognized as an independent state by the Great Powers.[51] [52] In return, Romania ceded three southern districts of Bessarabia to Russia and acquired Dobruja. In 1881, the principality was raised to a kingdom and Prince Carol became King Carol I.

The 1878–1914 period was one of stability and progress for Romania. During the Second Balkan War, Romania joined Greece, Serbia, Montenegro and Turkey against Bulgaria, and in the peace Treaty of Bucharest (1913) Romania gained Southern Dobrudja.[53]

World Wars and Greater Romania

(1916–1945)

Main articles: Romanian Campaign (World War I), Greater Romania, and Romania during World War II

In August 1914, when World War I broke out, Romania declared neutrality. Two years later, under pressure from the Allies (especially France, desperate to open a new front), on August 14/27 1916, Romania joined the Allies, declaring war on Austria-Hungary. For this action, under the terms of the secret military convention, Romania was promised support for its goal of national unity for all Romanian people.[54]

The Romanian military campaign ended in disaster for Romania as the Central Powers conquered two-thirds of the country and captured or killed the majority of its army within four months. Nevertheless, Moldavia remained in Romanian hands after the invading forces were stopped in 1917. By the war's end, Austria-Hungary and the Russian Empire had collapsed and disintegrated; Bessarabia, Bukovina and Transylvania proclaimed unions with the Kingdom of Romania in 1918. Total deaths from 1914 to 1918,

Romanian territory during the 20th century: purple indicates the Old Kingdom before 1913, pink indicates Greater Romania areas that joined after WWI and remained so after WWII, and orange indicates areas that joined Romania after WWI or were annexed after the Second Balkan War, but were lost after WWII. The small Hertza region, also purple but delimited, was part of the Old Kingdom before 1913, but was lost after WWII.

military and civilian, within contemporary borders, were estimated at 748,000.[55] By the 1920 Treaty of Trianon, Hungary renounced in favour of Romania all the claims of the Austro-Hungarian Monarchy over Transylvania.[56] The union of Romania with Bukovina was ratified in 1919 in the Treaty of Saint Germain,[57] and with Bessarabia in 1920 by the Treaty of Paris.[58]

The Romanian expression România Mare (literal translation "Great Romania", but more commonly rendered "Greater Romania") generally refers to the Romanian state in the interwar period, and by extension, to the territory Romania covered at the time (see map). Romania achieved at that time its greatest territorial extent (almost 300000 km^2/120000 sq mi),[59] managing to unite all the historic Romanian lands.[59]

During the Second World War, Romania tried again to remain neutral, but on June 28, 1940, it received a Soviet ultimatum with an implied threat of invasion in the event of non-compliance.[60] Under pressure from Moscow and Berlin, the Romanian administration and the army were forced to retreat from Bessarabia as well from Northern Bukovina to avoid war.[61] This, in combination with other factors, prompted the government to join the Axis. Thereafter, southern Dobruja was awarded to Bulgaria, while Hungary received Northern Transylvania as result of an Axis arbitration.[62] The authoritarian King Carol II

Romanian Army tanks entering Chişinău in 1941

abdicated in 1940, succeeded by the National Legionary State, in which power was shared by Ion Antonescu and the Iron Guard. Within months, Antonescu had crushed the Iron Guard, and the subsequent year Romania entered the war on the side of the Axis powers. During the war, Romania was the most important source of oil for Nazi Germany,[63] which attracted multiple bombing raids by the Allies. By means of the Axis invasion of the Soviet

Union, Romania recovered Bessarabia and northern Bukovina from the Soviet Russia, under the leadership of general Ion Antonescu. The Antonescu regime played a major role in the Holocaust,[64] following to a lesser extent the Nazi policy of oppression and massacre of the Jews, and Romas, primarily in the Eastern territories Romania recovered or occupied from the Soviet Union (Transnistria) and in Moldavia.[65]

In August 1944, Antonescu was toppled and arrested by King Michael I of Romania. Romania changed sides and joined the Allies, but its role in the defeat of Nazi Germany was not recognized by the Paris Peace Conference of 1947.[66] By the end of the war, the Romanian army had suffered about 300,000 casualties.[67] Jewish Holocaust victims totaled 469,000 within the 1939 borders, including 325,000 in Bessarabia and Bukovina.[68]

Communism

(1945–1989)

Main article: → Communist Romania

With Red Army forces still stationed in the country and exerting *de facto* control, the Communist-dominated government called new elections, which were won with 80% of the vote through intimidation and likely electoral fraud.[69] They thus rapidly established themselves as the dominant political force.

In 1947, the Communists forced King Michael I to abdicate and leave the country, and proclaimed Romania a people's republic.[70] [71] Romania remained under the direct military occupation and economic control of the USSR until the late 1950s. During this period, Romania's vast natural resources were continuously drained [72] by mixed Soviet-Romanian companies (SovRoms) set up for exploitative purposes.[73] [74]

The coat of arms of the Romanian Communist Party

From the late 1940s to the early 1960s, the Communist government established a reign of terror, carried out mainly through the Securitate (the new secret police). During this time they launched several campaigns to eliminate "enemies of the state", in which numerous individuals were killed or imprisoned for arbitrary political or economic reasons.[75] Punishment included deportation, internal exile, and internment in forced labour camps and prisons; dissent was vigorously suppressed. A notorious experiment in this period took place in the Pitești prison, where a group of political opponents were put into a program of reeducation through torture. Historical records show hundreds of thousands of abuses, deaths and incidents of torture against a wide range of people, from political opponents to ordinary citizens.[76]

In 1965, → Nicolae Ceaușescu came to power and started to pursue independent policies such as being the only Warsaw Pact country to condemn the Soviet-led 1968 invasion of Czechoslovakia, and to continue diplomatic relations with Israel after the Six-Day War of 1967; establishing economic (1963) and diplomatic (1967) relations with the Federal Republic of Germany.[77] Also, close ties with the Arab countries (and the PLO) allowed Romania to play a key role in the Israel–Egypt and Israel–PLO peace processes.[78] But as Romania's foreign debt sharply increased between 1977 and 1981 (from 3 to 10 billion US dollars),[79] the influence of international financial organisations such as the IMF or the World Bank grew, conflicting with → Nicolae Ceaușescu's autarchic policies. He eventually initiated a project of total reimbursement of the foreign debt by imposing policies that impoverished Romanians and exhausted the Romanian economy, while also greatly extending the authority of the police state, and imposing a cult of personality. These led to a dramatic decrease in Ceaușescu's popularity and culminated in his overthrow and execution in the bloody → Romanian Revolution of 1989.

In 2006, the Presidential Commission for the Study of the Communist Dictatorship in Romania estimated the number of direct victims of communist repression at two million people.[80] [81] This number does not include people who died in liberty as a result of their treatment in communist prisons, nor does it include people who died because of the dire economic circumstances in which the country found itself.

Present-day democracy

Main article: → History of Romania since 1989

After the revolution, the National Salvation Front, led by Ion Iliescu, took partial multi-party democratic and free market measures.[82] [83] Several major political parties of the pre-war era, such as the Christian-Democratic National Peasants' Party, the National Liberal Party and the Romanian Social Democrat Party were resurrected. After several major political rallies, in April 1990, a sit-in protest contesting the results of the recently held parliamentary elections began in University Square, Bucharest accusing the Front of being made up of former Communists and members of the Securitate. The protesters did not recognize the results of the election, deeming them undemocratic, and asked for the exclusion from the political life of the former high-ranking Communist Party members. The protest rapidly grew to become an ongoing mass demonstration (known as the Golaniad). The peaceful demonstrations degenerated into violence, and the violent intervention of coal miners from the Jiu Valley led to what is remembered as the June 1990 Mineriad.[84]

The subsequent disintegration of the Front produced several political parties including the Romanian Democrat Social Party (later Social Democratic Party), the Democratic Party and the (Alliance for Romania). The first governed Romania from 1990 until 1996 through several coalitions and governments and with Ion Iliescu as head of state. Since then there have been three democratic changes of government: in 1996, the democratic-liberal opposition and its leader Emil Constantinescu acceded to power; in 2000 the Social Democrats returned to power, with Iliescu once again president; and in 2004 Traian Băsescu was elected president, with an electoral coalition called Justice and Truth Alliance. The government was formed by a larger coalition which also includes the Conservative Party and the ethnic Hungarian party.

Post-Cold War Romania developed closer ties with Western Europe, eventually joining NATO in 2004, and hosting in Bucharest the 2008 summit.[85] The country applied in June 1993 for membership in the European Union and became an Associated State of the EU in 1995, an Acceding Country in 2004, and a member on January 1, 2007.[86]

See also: Accession of Romania to the European Union

Following the free travel agreement and politic of the post-Cold War period, as well as hardship of the life in the post 1990s economic depression, Romania has an increasingly large diaspora, estimated at over 2 million people. The main emigration targets are Spain, Italy, Germany, Austria, UK, Canada and the USA.[87]

Geography

Main article: Geography of Romania

With a surface area of 238391 square kilometres (92043 sq mi), Romania is the largest country in southeastern Europe and the twelfth-largest in Europe.[88] A large part of Romania's border with Serbia and Bulgaria is formed by the Danube. The Danube is joined by the Prut River, which forms the border with the Republic of Moldova.[88] The Danube flows into the Black Sea within Romania's territory forming the Danube Delta, the second largest and the best preserved delta in Europe, and a biosphere reserve and a biodiversity World Heritage Site.[89] Other important rivers are the Siret, running north-south through Moldavia, the Olt, running from the oriental Carpathian Mountains to Oltenia, and the Mureş, running through Transylvania from East to West.[88]

Topographic map of Romania

Romania's terrain is distributed roughly equally between mountainous, hilly and lowland territories. The Carpathian Mountains dominate the center of Romania, with fourteen of its mountain ranges reaching above the altitude of 2,000 meters.[88] The highest mountain in Romania is Moldoveanu Peak (2544 m/8350 ft). In south-central Romania, the Carpathians sweeten into hills, towards the Bărăgan Plains. Romania's geographical diversity has led to an accompanying diversity of flora and fauna.[88]

Environment

Main article: Protected areas in Romania

A high percentage (47% of the land area) of the country is covered with natural and semi-natural ecosystems.[90] Since almost half of all forests in Romania (13% of the country) have been managed for watershed conservation rather than production, Romania has one of the largest areas of undisturbed forest in Europe.[90] The integrity of Romanian forest ecosystems is indicated by the presence of the full range of European forest fauna, including 60% and 40% of all European brown bears and wolves, respectively.[91] There are also almost 400 unique species of mammals (of which Carpathian chamois are best known), birds, reptiles and amphibians in Romania.[92]

Glacial lakes within Retezat National Park

There are almost 10000 km^2 (3900 sq mi) (almost 5% of the total area) of protected areas in Romania.[93] Of these, Danube Delta Reserve Biosphere is the largest and least damaged wetland complex in Europe, covering a total area of 5800 km^2 (2200 sq mi).[94] The significance of the biodiversity of the Danube Delta has been internationally recognised. It was declared a Biosphere Reserve in September 1990, a Ramsar site in May 1991, and over 50% of its area was placed on the World Heritage List in December 1991.[95] Within its boundaries is one of the most extensive reed bed systems in the world.[96] There are two other biosphere reserves: Retezat National Park and Rodna National

Park.

Flora and fauna

Main articles: Flora of Romania and List of mammals of Romania

In Romania there have been identified 3,700 plant species from which to date 23 have been declared natural monuments, 74 missing, 39 are endangered, 171 vulnerable and 1,253 are considered rare.[97] The three major vegetation areas in Romania are the alpine zone, the forest zone and the steppe zone. The egetation is distributed in an storied manner in accordance with the characteristics of soil and climate, but according to altitude as: oak, flasks, linden, ash (in the steppe zone and low hills), beech, oak (between 500 and 1200 meters), spruce, fir, pine (between 1200 and 1800 m), juniper, Mountain Pine and dwarf trees (in 1800 and 2000 meters), alpine meadows consisting of small

Pelicans in the Danube Delta

herbs (over 2000 meters).[98] Off the high valleys, due to persistent moisture, there is a specific vegetation of meadow, reed, rush, sedge, and often with patches of willows, poplars and Arini. In the Danube Delta swamp vegetation is dominant.[98]

The fauna of Romania consists of 33,792 species of animals, 33,085 invertebrate and 707 vertebrate.[97] The vertebrate species consist of 191 fish, 20 amphibian, 30 reptile, 364 bird and 102 mammal species.[97] Fauna is especially broken down by vegetation. Thus, specific floor steppe and forest steppe have the following species: rabbit, hamster, ground squirrel, pheasant, drop, quail, carp, perch, pike, catfish, the forest floor of hardwood (oak and beech): boar, wolf, fox, barbel, woodpecker, and for coniferous forest floor: trout, lynx, deer, goats and specific alpine fauna like black and bald eagles.[98] In particular the Danube Delta is the place where hundreds of species of birds exist, including pelicans, swans, wild geese and flamingos, birds that are protected by law. The delta is also a seasonal stopover for migratory birds. Some rare species of birds in the Dobrogea area are the pelican, cormorant, little deer, Red-breasted Goose, White-fronted Goose and the Mute Swan.[99]

Climate

Main article: Climate of Romania

Owing to its distance from the open sea and position on the southeastern portion of the European continent, Romania has a climate that is transitional between temperate and continental with four distinct seasons. The average annual temperature is 11 °C (52 °F) in the south and 8 °C (46 °F) in the north.[100] The extreme recorded temperatures are 44.5 °C (112.1 °F) in Ion Sion 1951 and −38.5 °C (−37 °F) in Bod 1942.[101]

Spring is pleasant with cool mornings and nights and warm days. Summers are generally very warm to hot, with summer (June to August) average maximum temperatures in Bucharest being around 28 °C (82 °F),[102] with temperatures over 35 °C (95 °F) fairly common in the lower-lying areas of the country. Minima in Bucharest and other lower-lying areas are around 16 °C (61 °F), but at higher altitudes both maxima and minima decline considerably. Autumn is dry and cool, with fields and trees producing colorful foliage. Winters can be cold, with average maxima even in lower-lying areas being no more than 2 °C (36 °F) and below −15 °C (5.0 °F) in the highest mountains, where some areas of permafrost occur on the highest peaks.[103]

Precipitation is average with over 750 mm (30 in) per year only on the highest western mountains — much of it falling as snow which allows for an extensive skiing industry. In the south-centern parts of the country (around

Bucharest) the level of precipitation drops to around 600 mm (24 in),[104] while in the Danube Delta, rainfall levels are very low, and average only around 370 mm.

Demographics

Main article: Demographics of Romania

According to the 2002 census, Romania has a population of 21,698,181 and, similarly to other countries in the region, is expected to gently decline in the coming years as a result of sub-replacement fertility rates. Romanians make up 89.5% of the population. The largest ethnic minorities are Hungarians, who make up 6.6% of the population and Roma, or Gypsies, who make up 2.46% of the population. By the official census 535,250 Roma live in Romania.[105] [106] Hungarians, who are a sizeable minority in

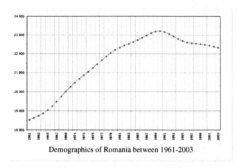

Demographics of Romania between 1961-2003

Transylvania, constitute a majority in the counties of Harghita and Covasna. Ukrainians, Germans, Lipovans, Turks, Tatars, Serbs, Slovaks, Bulgarians, Croats, Greeks, Russians, Jews, Czechs, Poles, Italians, Armenians, as well as other ethnic groups, account for the remaining 1.4% of the population.[107] Of the 745,421 Germans in Romania in 1930,[108] only about 60,000 remained.[109] In 1924, there were 796,056 Jews in the Kingdom of Romania.[110] The number of Romanians and individuals with ancestors born in Romania living abroad is estimated at around 12 million.[87]

The official language of Romania is Romanian, an Eastern Romance language related to Italian, French, Spanish, Portuguese and Catalan. Romanian is spoken as a first language by 91% of the population, with Hungarian and Rroma, being the most important minority languages, spoken by 6.7% and 1.1% of the population, respectively.[107] Until the 1990s, there was also a substantial number of German-speaking Transylvanian Saxons, even though many have since emigrated to Germany, leaving only 45,000 native German speakers in Romania. In localities where a given ethnic minority makes up more than 20% of the population, that minority's language can be used in the public administration and justice system, while native-language education and signage is also provided. English and French are the main foreign languages taught in schools. English is spoken by 5 million Romanians, French is spoken by 4–5 million, and German, Italian and Spanish are each spoken by 1–2 million people.[111] Historically, French was the predominant foreign language spoken in Romania, even though English has since superseded it. Consequently, Romanian English-speakers tend to be younger than Romanian French-speakers. Romania is, however, a full member of La Francophonie, and hosted the Francophonie Summit in 2006.[112] German has been taught predominantly in Transylvania, due to traditions tracing back to the Austro-Hungarian rule in this province.

Religion

Main articles: Religion in Romania and Romanian Orthodox Church

Romania is a secular state, thus having no national religion. The dominant religious body is the Romanian Orthodox Church, an autocephalous church within the Eastern Orthodox communion; its members make up 86.7% of the population according to the 2002 census. Other important Christian denominations include Roman Catholicism (4.7%), Protestantism (3.7%), Pentecostalism (1.5%) and the Romanian Greek-Catholic Church (0.9%).[107] Romania also has a Muslim minority concentrated in Dobrogea, mostly of Turkish ethnicity and numbering 67,500 people.[113] Based on the 2002 census data, there are also 6,179 Jews, 23,105 people who are of no religion and/or atheist, and 11,734 who refused to answer. On December 27, 2006, a new Law on Religion was approved under which religious denominations can only receive official registration if they have at least 20,000 members, or about

0.1 percent of Romania's total population.[114]

Largest cities

Main article: Metropolitan areas in Romania

Bucharest is the capital and the largest city in Romania. At the census in 2002, its population was over 1.9 million.[115] The metropolitan area of Bucharest has a population of about 2.2 million. There are several plans to increase further its metropolitan area to about 20 times the area of the city proper.[116] [117]

There are 5 more cities in Romania, with a population of around 300,000, that are also present in the EU's top 100 most populous cities. These are: Iaşi, Cluj-Napoca, Timişoara, Constanţa, and Craiova. The other cities with populations over 200,000 are Galaţi, Braşov, Ploieşti, Brăila and Oradea. Another 13 cities have populations over 100,000.[4]

Cluj-Napoca one of the largest Romanian cities

At present, several of the largest cities have a metropolitan area: Constanţa (550,000 people), Braşov, Iaşi (both with around 400,000) and Oradea (260,000) and several others are planned: Timişoara (400,000), Cluj-Napoca (400,000), Brăila-Galaţi (600,000), Craiova (370,000), Bacău and Ploieşti.[118]

Education

Main article: Romanian educational system

Since the → Romanian Revolution of 1989, the Romanian educational system has been in a continuous process of reform that has been both praised and criticized.[119] According to the Law on Education adopted in 1995, the educational system is regulated by the Ministry of Education and Research. Each level has its own form of organization and is subject to different legislation. Kindergarten is optional for children between 3 and 6 years old. Schooling starts at age 7 (sometimes 6), and is compulsory until the 10th grade (which usually corresponds to the age of 17 or 16).[120] Primary and secondary education are divided into 12 or 13 grades. Higher education is aligned with the European higher education area.

University of Bucharest main building

Aside from the official schooling system, and the recently-added private equivalents, there exists a semi-legal, informal, fully private tutoring system. Tutoring is mostly used during secondary as a preparation for the various examinations, which are notoriously difficult. Tutoring is widespread, and it can be considered a part of the Education System. It has subsisted and even prospered during the Communist regime.[121]

In 2004, some 4.4 million of the population was enrolled in school. Out of these, 650,000 in kindergarten, 3.11 million (14% of population) in primary and secondary level, and 650,000 (3% of population) in tertiary level (universities).[122] In the same year, the adult literacy rate was 97.3% (45th worldwide), while the combined gross enrollment ratio for primary, secondary and tertiary schools was 75% (52nd worldwide).[123] The results of the PISA assessment study in schools for the year 2000 placed Romania on the 34th rank out of 42 participant countries with a general weighted score of 432 representing 85% of the mean OECD score.[124] According to the Academic Ranking of World Universities, in 2006 no Romanian university was included in the first 500 top universities world wide.[125] Using similar methodology to these rankings, it was reported that the best placed Romanian university, Bucharest University, attained the half score of the last university in the world top 500.[126]

Romanian high school curricula have recently been censored and restructured, owing to a growing trend of religious conservatism. In 2006, the theory of evolution, which had been taught since the country's Communist era, was dropped from the compulsory curriculum nationwide. Philosophical writers critical of religion, such as Voltaire and Camus have also been removed from the philosophy curriculum. Instead, students are taught 7-day Creationism in Orthodox religion classes, which under new proposals could become compulsory.[127]

Government

Politics

Main article: Politics of Romania

The Constitution of Romania is based on the Constitution of France's Fifth Republic[128] and was approved in a national referendum on December 8, 1991.[128] A plebiscite held in October 2003 approved 79 amendments to the Constitution, bringing it into conformity with European Union legislation.[128] Romania is governed on the basis of multi-party democratic system and of the segregation of the legislative, executive and judicial powers.[128] Romania is a semi-presidential democratic republic where executive functions are shared between the president and the prime minister. The President is elected by popular vote for maximum two terms, and since the amendments in 2003, the terms are five years.[128] The

Palace of the Parliament

President appoints the Prime Minister, who in turn appoints the Council of Ministers.[128] While the president resides at Cotroceni Palace, the Prime Minister with the Romanian Government is based at Victoria Palace.

The legislative branch of the government, collectively known as the Parliament (*Parlamentul României*), consists of two chambers – the Senate (*Senat*), which has 140 members, and the Chamber of Deputies (*Camera Deputaţilor*), which has 346 members.[128] The members of both chambers are elected every four years under a system of party-list proportional representation.[128]

The justice system is independent of the other branches of government, and is made up of a hierarchical system of courts culminating in the High Court of Cassation and Justice, which is the supreme court of Romania.[129] There are also courts of appeal, county courts and local courts. The Romanian judicial system is strongly influenced by the French model,[128] [130] considering that it is based on civil law and is inquisitorial in nature. The Constitutional Court (*Curtea Constituţională*) is responsible for judging the compliance of laws and other state regulations to the Romanian Constitution, which is the fundamental law of the country. The constitution, which was introduced in 1991, can only be amended by a public referendum, the last one being in 2003. Since this amendment, the court's decisions cannot be overruled by any majority of the parliament.

The country's entry into the European Union in 2007 [131] has been a significant influence on its domestic policy. As part of the process, Romania has instituted reforms including judicial reform, increased judicial cooperation with other member states, and measures to combat corruption. Nevertheless, in 2006 Brussels report, Romania and Bulgaria were described as the two most corrupt countries in the EU.[132]

Administrative divisions

Main article: Administrative divisions of Romania

Romania is divided into forty-one counties (sing. *judeţ*, pl. *judeţe*), plus the municipality of Bucharest (Bucureşti) – which has equal rank. Each county is administered by a county council (*consiliu judeţean*), responsible for local affairs, as well as a prefect, who is appointed by the central government but cannot be a member of any political party, responsible for the administration of national (central) affairs at the county level. Since 2008, the president of the county council (*preşedintele consiliului judeţean*) is directly elected by the people, and not by the county council as before that.[133]

Map of the 8 development regions. The 41 local administrative units are also highlighted, but Bucharest and Ilfov county are lumped together. The two form a development region of their own, surrounded by the Sud region.

Each county is further subdivided into cities (sing. *oraş*, pl. *oraşe*) and communes (sing. *comună*, pl. *comune*), the former being urban, and the latter being rural localities. There are a total of 319 cities and 2686 communes in Romania.[134] Each city and commune has its own mayor (*primar*) and local council (*consiliu local*). 103 of the larger and more urbanised cities have the status of municipality, which gives them greater administrative power over local affairs. Bucharest is also reckoned as a city with municipality status, but it is unique among the other localities in that it is not part of a county. It does not have a county concil, but has a prefect. Bucharest elects a general mayor (*primar general*) and a general city council (*Consiliul General Bucureşti*). Each of Bucharest's six sectors also elects a mayor and a local council.[134]

The NUTS-3 level divisions reflect Romania's administrative-territorial structure, and correspond to the 41 counties, and the Bucharest municipality.[135] Cities and communes are NUTS-5 level divisions. The country currently does not have NUTS-4 level divisions, but there are plans to make such associating neighboring localities for better coordination of local development and assimilation of national and European funds.[135]

The 41 counties and Bucharest are grouped into eight development regions corresponding to NUTS-2 divisions in the European Union.[135] Prior to Romania's accession into the European Union, these were called statistical regions, and were used exclusively for statistical purposes. Thus, albeit they formally existed for over 40 years, the regions are publicly a news. There are proposals in the future to cancel county councils (but leave the prefects) and create regional councils instead. This would not change the nomenclature of the country's territorial subdivision, but would presumably allow better coordination of policy at the local level, more autonomy, and a smaller bureaucracy.[135]

There are also proposals to use four NUTS-1 level divisions; they would be called macroregions (Romanian:*Macroregiune*). NUTS-1 and -2 divisions have no administrative capacity and are instead used for co-ordinating regional development projects and statistical purposes.[135]

- Macroregiunea 1:[135]
  - Nord-Vest (6 counties; roughtly northern Transylvania)
  - Centru (6 counties; roughly southern Transylvania)

- Macroregiunea 2:[135]
  - Nord-Est (6 counties; Moldavia except the counties of Vrancea and Galaţi)
  - Sud-Est (6 counties; lower Danube, including Dobrudja)
- Macroregiunea 3:[135]
  - Sud (7 counties; the core of Muntenia)
  - Bucureşti (1 county and Bucharest)
- Macroregiunea 4:[135]
  - Sud-Vest (5 counties; roughly Oltenia)
  - Vest (4 counties; southwestern Transylvania, or Banat plus Arad and Hunedoara counties)

Foreign relations

Main article: Foreign relations of Romania

Since December 1989, Romania has pursued a policy of strengthening relations with the West in general, more specifically with the United States and the European Union. It joined the North Atlantic Treaty Organisation (NATO) on March 29, 2004, the European Union (EU) on January 1, 2007, and the International Monetary Fund and the World Bank in 1972, and is a member of the World Trade Organization.

The current government has stated its goal of strengthening ties with and helping other Eastern European countries (in particular Moldova, Ukraine and Georgia) with the process of integration with the West.[136] Romania has also made clear since the late 1990s that it supports NATO and EU membership for the democratic former Soviet republics in Eastern Europe and the Caucasus.[136] Romania also declared its public support for Turkey, Croatia and Moldova joining the European Union.[136] With Turkey, Romania shares a privileged economic relation.[137] Because it has a large Hungarian minority, Romania has also developed strong relations with Hungary – the latter supported Romania's bid to join the EU.[138]

In December 2005, President Traian Băsescu and United States Secretary of State Condoleezza Rice signed an agreement that would allow a U.S. military presence at several Romanian facilities primarily in the eastern part of the country.[139] In May 2009, the American state secretary Hillary Clinton declared that "Romania is one of the most trustworthy and respectable partners of the USA" during a visit of the Romanian foreign minister.[140]

Relations with Moldova are special,[136] considering that the two countries practically share the same language, and a fairly common historical background. A movement for unification of Romania and Moldova appeared in the early 1990s after both countries achieved emancipation from communist rule,[141] but quickly faded away with the new Moldovan government that had an agenda to preserve a Moldovan republic independent of Romania.[142] Romania remains interested in Moldovan affairs and has officially rejected the Molotov-Ribbentrop Pact,[141] but the two countries have been unable even to reach agreement on a basic bilateral treaty.[143]

Armed Forces

Main article: Romanian Armed Forces

The Romanian Armed Forces consist of Land, Air, and Naval Forces, and are led by a Commander-in-chief who is managed by the Ministry of Defense. The president is the Supreme Commander of the Armed Forces during wartime. Of the 90,000 men and women which the Armed Forces comprise, 15,000 are civilians and 75,000 are military personnel—45,800 for land, 13,250 for air, 6,800 for naval forces, and 8,800 in other fields.[144]

Romanian Army soldiers in Afghanistan

The total defence spending currently accounts for 2.05% of total national GDP, which represents approximately 2.9 billion dollars (ranked 39th). However, the Romanian Armed Forces will spend about 11 billion dollars between 2006 and 2011, for modernization and acquisition of new equipment.[145] The Land Forces have overhauled their equipment in the past few years, and today are an army with multiple NATO capabilities, participating in a NATO peacekeeping mission in Afghanistan. The Air Force currently operates modernized Soviet MiG-21LanceR fighters which are due to be replaced by new advanced 4.5 generation Western jet fighters, such as the F-16 Fighting Falcon, Eurofighter Typhoon or JAS 39 Gripen.[146] Also, in order to replace the bulk of the old transport force, the Air Force ordered seven new C-27J Spartan tactical airlift aircraft which are to be delivered starting with late 2008.[147] Two modernized ex-Royal Navy Type 22 frigates were acquired by the Naval Forces in 2004, and a further four modern missile corvettes will be commissioned until 2010.

Economy

Main article: Economy of Romania

With a GDP of around $264 billion and a GDP per capita (PPP) of $12,285[148] estimated for 2008, Romania is an upper-middle income country economy[149] and has been part of the European Union since January 1, 2007. After the → Communist regime was → overthrown in late 1989, the country experienced a decade of economic instability and decline, led in part by an obsolete industrial base and a lack of structural reform. From 2000 onwards, however, the Romanian economy was transformed into one of relative macroeconomic stability, characterised by high growth, low unemployment and declining inflation. In 2006, according to the Romanian Statistics Office, GDP growth in real terms was recorded at

ArcelorMittal steel mill in Galaţi

7.7%, one of the highest rates in Europe.[150] Growth dampened to 6.1% in 2007,[151] but was expected to exceed 8% in 2008 because of a high production forecast in agriculture (30–50% higher than in 2007). The GDP grew by 8.9% in the first nine months of 2008, but growth fell to 2.9% in the fourth quarter and stood at 7.1% for the whole 2008 because of the financial crisis.[152] According to Eurostat data, the Romanian PPS GDP per capita stood at 46 per cent of the EU average in 2008.[153] Unemployment in Romania was at 3.9% in September 2007,[154] which is very low compared to other middle-sized or large European countries such as Poland, France, Germany and Spain. Foreign debt is also comparatively low, at 20.3% of GDP.[155] Exports have increased substantially in the past few years, with a 25% year-on-year rise in exports in the first quarter of 2006. Romania's main exports are clothing and textiles, industrial machinery, electrical and electronic equipment, metallurgic products, raw materials, cars, military equipment, software, pharmaceuticals, fine chemicals, and agricultural products (fruits, vegetables, and flowers). Trade is mostly centred on the member states of the European Union, with Germany and Italy being the country's single largest trading partners. The country, however, maintains a large trade deficit, which increased sharply during 2007 by 50%, to €15 billon.[156]

After a series of privatisations and reforms in the late 1990s and early 2000s, government intervention in the Romanian economy is somewhat lower than in other European economies.[157] In 2005, the government replaced Romania's progressive tax system with a flat tax of 16% for both personal income and corporate profit, resulting in the country having the lowest fiscal burden in the European Union,[158] a factor which has contributed to the growth of the private sector. The economy is predominantly based on services, which account for 55% of GDP, even though industry and agriculture also have significant contributions, making up 35% and 10% of GDP, respectively. Additionally, 32% of the Romanian population is employed in agriculture and primary production, one of the highest rates in Europe.[155] Since 2000, Romania has attracted increasing amounts of foreign investment, becoming the single largest investment destination in Southeastern and Central Europe. Foreign direct investment was valued at €8.3 billion in 2006.[159] According to a 2006 World Bank report, Romania currently ranks 49th out of 175 economies in the ease of doing business, scoring higher than other countries in the region such as Hungary and the Czech Republic.[160] Additionally, the same study judged it to be the world's second-fastest economic reformer (after Georgia) in 2006.[161] The average gross wage per month in Romania was 1855 lei in May 2009,[162] equating to €442.48 (US$627.70) based on international exchange rates, and $1110.31 based on purchasing power parity.[163]

Transportation

Main article: Transport in Romania

Due to its location, Romania is a major crossroad for International economic exchange in Europe. However, because of insufficient investment, maintenance and repair, the transport infrastructure does not meet the current needs of a market economy and lags behind Western Europe.[164] Nevertheless, these conditions are rapidly improving and catching up with the standards of Trans-European transport networks. Several projects have been started with funding from grants from ISPA and several loans from International Financial Institutions (World Bank, IMF, etc.) guaranteed by the state, to upgrade the main road corridors. Also, the Government is actively pursuing new external financing or public-private partnerships to further upgrade the main roads, and especially the country's motorway network.[164]

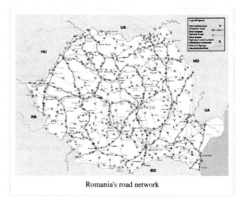

Romania's road network

The World Bank estimates that the railway network in Romania comprised in 2004 22298 kilometres (13855 mi) of track, which would make it the fourth largest railroad network in Europe.[165] The railway transport experienced a dramatic fall in freight and passenger volumes from the peak volumes recorded in 1989 mainly due to the decline in GDP and competition from road transport. In 2004, the railways carried 8.64 billion passenger-km in 99 million passenger journeys, and 73 million metric tonnes, or 17 billion ton-km of freight.[128] The combined total transportation by rail constituted around 45% of all passenger and freight movement in the country.[128]

Bucharest is the only city in Romania which has an underground railway system. The Bucharest Metro was only opened in 1979 and is now one of the most accessed systems of the Bucharest public transport network with an average ridership of 600,000 passengers during the workweek.[166]

Tourism

Main article: Tourism in Romania

Tourism focuses on the country's natural landscapes and its rich history and is a significant contributor to the Romania's economy. In 2006, the domestic and international tourism generated about 4.8% of gross domestic product and 5.8% of the total jobs (about half a million jobs).[167] Following commerce, tourism is the second largest component of the services sector. Tourism is one of the most dynamic and fastest developing sectors of the economy of Romania and characterized by a huge potential for development. According to the World Travel and Tourism Council Romania is the fourth fastest growing country in the world in terms of travel and tourism total demand with

Mamaia Resort at the Black Sea shore

a yearly potential growth of 8% from 2007-2016.[168] Number of tourists grew from 4.8 million in 2002 to 6.6 million in 2004.[128] Similarly, the revenues grew from 400 million in 2002 to 607 in 2004.[128] In 2006, Romania registered 20 million overnight stays by international tourists, an all-time record,[169] but the number for 2007 is expected to increase even more.[170] Tourism in Romania attracted €400 million in investments in 2005.[171]

Over the last years, Romania has emerged as a popular tourist destination for many Europeans (more than 60% of the foreign visitors were from EU countries),[170] thus attempting to compete with Bulgaria, Greece, Italy and Spain. Romania destinations such as Mangalia, Saturn, Venus, Neptun, Olimp, Constanta and Mamaia (sometimes called the *Romanian Riviera*) are among the most popular attraction during summer.[172] During winter, the skiing resorts along the Valea Prahovei and Poiana Braşov are popular with foreign visitors. For their medieval atmosphere and castles, Transylvanian cities such as Sibiu, Braşov, Sighişoara, Cluj-Napoca, Târgu Mureş have become important touristic attractions for foreigners. Rural tourism focused on

A view from the Carpathian Mountains near Prahova Valley

folklore and traditions, has become an important alternative recently,[173] and is targeted to promote such sites as Bran and its Dracula's Castle, the Painted churches of Northern Moldavia, the Wooden churches of Maramureş, or the Merry Cemetery in Maramureş County.[174] Other major natural attractions in Romania such as Danube Delta,[128] Iron Gates (Danube Gorge), Scărişoara Cave and several other caves in the Apuseni Mountains have yet to receive great attention.

Culture

Main article: Culture of Romania

Romania has its unique culture, which is the product of its geography and of its distinct historical evolution. Like Romanians themselves, it is fundamentally defined as the meeting point of three regions: Central Europe, Eastern Europe, and the Balkans, but cannot be truly included in any of them.[175] The Romanian identity formed on a substratum of mixed Roman and quite possibly Dacian elements,[176] with many other influences. During late Antiquity and the Middle Ages, the major influences came from the Slavic peoples who migrated and settled in near Romania;[176] from medieval Greeks,[176] and the Byzantine Empire;[177] from a long domination by the Ottoman Empire;[178] from the Hungarians;[176] and from the Germans living in Transylvania. Modern Romanian culture emerged

The Palace of Culture in Iaşi was built between 1906 and 1925 and hosts several museums

and developed over roughly the last 250 years under a strong influence from Western culture, particularly French,[177] and German culture.[177]

Arts

Main articles: Literature of Romania, Music of Romania, Arts in Romania, Cinema of Romania, and Romanian philosophy

The Romanian literature began to truly evolve with the revolutions of 1848 and the union of the two Danubian Principalities in 1859. The Origin of the Romanians began to be discussed and in Transylvania and Romanian scholars began studying in France, Italy and Germany.[177] The German philosophy and French culture were integrated into modern Romanian literature and a new elite of artists led to the appearance of some of the classics of the Romanian literature such as Mihai Eminescu, George Coşbuc, Ioan Slavici. Although they remain little known outside Romania, they are very appreciated within Romania for giving birth to a true Romanian literature by creating modern lyrics with inspiration from the old folklore tales. Of

Romanian Athenaeum in Bucharest was opened in 1888

them, Eminescu is considered the most important and influential Romanian poet, and is still very much loved for his creations, and especially the poem *Luceafărul*.[179] Among other writers that made large contributions around the second half of 19th century are Mihail Kogălniceanu (also the first prime minister of Romania), Vasile Alecsandri, Nicolae Bălcescu, Ion Luca Caragiale, and Ion Creangă.

The first half of the 20th century is regarded by many Romanian scholars as the *Golden Age* of Romanian culture and it is the period when it reached its main level of international affirmation and a strong connection to the European cultural trends.[180] The most important artist who had a great influence on the world culture was the sculptor Constantin Brâncuşi, a central figure of the modern movement and a pioneer of abstraction, the innovator of world sculpture by immersion in the primordial sources of folk creation. His sculptures blend simplicity and sophistication that led the way for modernist sculptors.[181] As a testimony to his skill, one of his pieces, *"Bird in Space"*, was sold in an auction for $27.5 million in 2005, a record for any sculpture.[182] [183] In the period between the two world wars, authors like Tudor Arghezi, Lucian Blaga, Eugen Lovinescu, Ion Barbu, Liviu Rebreanu made efforts to synchronize Romanian literature with the European literature of the time. From this period comes also George Enescu, probably the best known Romanian musician.[184] He is a composer, violinist, pianist, conductor, teacher, and one of the greatest performers of his time,[185] in whose honor is held the annually in Bucharest, the classical music George Enescu Festival.

Brâncuşi's *Endless Column* in Târgu Jiu

After the world wars, communism brought heavy censorship and used the cultural world as a means to better control the population. The freedom of expression was constantly restricted in various ways, but the likes of Gellu Naum, Nichita Stănescu, Marin Sorescu or Marin Preda managed to escape censorship, broke with "socialist realism" and were the leaders of a small "Renaissance" in Romanian literature.[186] While not many of them managed to obtain international acclaim due to the censorship, some like Constantin Noica, Tristan Tzara and Mircea Cărtărescu had their works published abroad even though they got jailed for various political reasons.

Some artists chose to leave the country entirely, and continued to make contributions in exile. Among them Eugen Ionescu, Mircea Eliade and Emil Cioran became renown worldwide for their works. Other literary figures who enjoy acclaim outside of the country include the poet Paul Celan and Nobel laureate Elie Wiesel, both survivors of the Holocaust. Some famous Romanian artists musicians are the folk artist Tudor Gheorghe, and the virtuoso of the pan flute Gheorghe Zamfir − who is reported to have sold over 120 million albums worldwide.[187] [188]

Romanian cinema has recently achieved worldwide acclaim with the appearance of such films as *The Death of Mr. Lazarescu*, directed by Cristi Puiu, (Cannes 2005 Prix un certain regard winner), and *4 Months, 3 Weeks and 2 Days*, directed by Cristian Mungiu (Cannes 2007 *Palme d'Or* winner).[189] The latter, according to *Variety*, is "further proof of Romania's new prominence in the film world."[190]

Monuments

See also: List of castles in Romania, List of museums in Romania, and UNESCO World Heritage Sites in Romania

The UNESCO List of World Heritage Sites[191] includes Romanian sites such as the Saxon villages with fortified churches in Transylvania, the Painted churches of northern Moldavia with their fine exterior and interior frescoes, the Wooden Churches of Maramures unique examples that combine Gothic style with traditional timber construction, the Monastery of Horezu, the citadel of Sighişoara, and the Dacian Fortresses of the Orăştie Mountains.[192] Romania's contribution to the World Heritage List stands out because it consists of some groups of monuments scattered around the country, rather than one or two special landmarks.[193] Also, in 2007, the city of Sibiu famous for its Brukenthal National Museum is the European Capital of Culture alongside the city of Luxembourg.

Sarmizegetusa Regia one of the six Dacian fortresses declared
UNESCO World Heritage Sites in Romania

National Flag

Main article: Flag of Romania

The national flag of Romania is a tricolour with vertical stripes: beginning from the flagpole, blue, yellow and red. It has a width-length ratio of 2:3. Romania's national flag is very similar to that of Chad.[194] [195] [196]

Sports

Main article: Sport in Romania

Football (soccer) is by far the most popular sport in Romania.[197] The governing body is the Romanian Football Federation, which belongs to UEFA. The top division of the Romanian Professional Football League attracted an average of 5417 spectators per game in the 2006–07 season.[198] At international level, the Romanian National Football Team has taken part 7 times in the Football World Cup, and it had the most successful period throughout the 1990s, when during the 1994 World Cup in the United States, Romania reached the quarter-finals and was ranked by FIFA on the 6th place. The core player of this "Golden Generation"[199] and perhaps the best known Romanian player internationally is Gheorghe Hagi (nicknamed *the Maradona of the Carpathians*).[200] Famous currently active players are Adrian Mutu and Cristian Chivu. The most famous football club is Steaua București, who in 1986 became the first Eastern European club ever to win the prestigious European Champions Cup title, and who played the final again in 1989. Another successful Romanian team Dinamo București played a semifinal in the European Champions Cup in 1984 and a Cup Winners Cup semifinal in the 1990. Other important Romanian football clubs are Rapid București, CFR 1907 Cluj-Napoca and FC Universitatea Craiova.

Nadia Comăneci (Right) with Condoleezza Rice (Left)

Tennis is the second most popular sport in terms of registered sportsmen.[197] Romania reached the Davis Cup finals three times (1969, 1971, 1972). The tennis player Ilie Năstase won several Grand Slam titles and dozens of other tournaments, and was the first player to be ranked as number 1 by ATP from 1973 to 1974. The Romanian Open is held every fall in Bucharest since 1993.

Popular team sports are rugby union (national rugby team has so far competed at every Rugby World Cup), basketball and handball.[197] Some popular individual sports are: athletics, chess, sport dance, and martial arts and other fighting sports.[197]

Romanian gymnastics has had a large number of successes – for which the country became known worldwide.[201] In the 1976 Summer Olympics, the gymnast Nadia Comăneci became the first gymnast ever to score a perfect ten. She also won three gold medals, one silver and one bronze, all at the age of fifteen.[202] Her success continued in the 1980 Summer Olympics, where she was awarded two gold medals and two silver medals.

Romania participated in for the first time in the Olympic Games in 1900 and has taken part in 18 of the 24 summer games. Romania has been one of the more successful countries at the Summer Olympic Games (15th overall) with a total of 283 medals won throughout the years, 82 of which are gold medals.[203] Winter sports have received little investments and thus only a single bronze medal was won by Romanian sportsmen in the Winter Olympic Games.

See also

Main article: Outline of Romania

* Index of Romania-related articles
* List of Romania-related topics

References

[1] " Populaţia stabilă la 1.01.2009 (http://www.insse.ro/cms/rw/resource/populatia stabila la 1 ianuarie 2009 si 18.xls?download=true)" (in Romanian). INSSE. May 19, 2009. . Retrieved May 20, 2009.

[2] " Romania (http://www.imf.org/external/pubs/ft/weo/2009/01/weodata/weorept.aspx?sy=2006&ey=2009&scsm=1&ssd=1& sort=country&ds=.&br=1&c=968&s=NGDPD,NGDPDPC,PPPGDP,PPPPC,LP&grp=0&a=&pr.x=40&pr.y=8)". International Monetary Fund. . Retrieved 2009-04-22.

[3] *North Atlantic Treaty Organization* (http://www.nato.int/invitees2004/romania/glance.htm). NATO. Report. Retrieved on 2008-08-31.

[4] " Romanian Statistical Yearbook (http://www.insse.ro/cms/files/pdf/en/cp2.pdf)" (PDF). Romanian National Institute of Statistics. 2007. . Retrieved 2008-01-20.

[5] " Report on the Nominations from Luxembourg and Romania for the European Capital of Culture 2007 (http://ec.europa.eu/culture/pdf/ doc670_en.pdf)" (pdf). The Selection Panel for the European Capital of Culture (ECOC) 2007. 2004-04-05. . Retrieved 2008-08-31.

[6] Explanatory Dictionary of the Romanian Language, 1998; New Explanatory Dictionary of the Romanian Language, 2002 (http://dexonline. ro/search.php?cuv=romÃ¢n)

[7] Andreas Verres. *Acta et Epistolae*. I. pp. 243. ""nunc se Romanos vocant""

[8] Cl. Isopescu (1929). "Notizie intorno ai romeni nella letteratura geografica italiana del Cinquecento". *Bulletin de la Section Historique* **XVI**: 1–90. ""...si dimandano in lingua loro Romei...se alcuno dimanda se sano parlare in la lingua valacca, dicono a questo in questo modo: Sti Rominest ? Che vol dire: Sai tu Romano,...".

[9] Maria Holban (1983) (in Romanian). *Călători străini despre Ţările Române*. II. Ed. Ştiinţifică şi Enciclopedică. pp. 158–161. ""Anzi essi si chiamano romanesci, e vogliono molti che erano mandati qui quei che erano dannati a cavar metalli...""

[10] Paul Cernovodeanu (1960) (in Romanian). *Voyage fait par moy, Pierre Lescalopier l'an 1574 de Venise a Constantinople, fol 48*. IV. 444. ""Tout ce pays la Wallachie et Moldavie et la plus part de la Transivanie a este peuple des colonie romaines du temps de Traian l'empereur...Ceux du pays se disent vrais successeurs des Romains et nomment leur parler romanechte, c'est-a-dire romain ... ""

[11] Iorga, N.. Hurmuzachi, Apud. ed. *Neacsu's Letter from Campulung* (http://cimec.ro/Istorie/neacsu/rom/scrisoare.htm). **Documente**, **XI**. pp. 843. . Retrieved 2008-08-31.

[12] *"am scris aceste sfente cărţi de învăţături, să fie popilor rumânesti... să înţeleagă toţi oamenii cine-s rumâni creştini"* "Întrebare creştinească" (1559), Bibliografia românească veche, IV, 1944, p. 6.

"...că văzum cum toate limbile au şi înfluresc întru cuvintele slăvite a lui Dumnezeu numai noi românii pre limbă nu avem. Pentru aceia cu mare muncă scoasem de limba jidovească si grecească si srâbească pre limba românească 5 cărţi ale lui Moisi prorocul si patru cărţi şi le dăruim voo fraţi rumâni şi le-au scris în cheltuială multă... şi le-au dăruit voo fraţilor români,... şi le-au scris voo fraţilor români" Palia de la Orăştie (1581–1582), Bucureşti, 1968.

În Ţara Ardealului nu lăcuiesc numai unguri, ce şi saşi peste seamă de mulţi şi români peste tot locul..., Grigore Ureche, Letopiseţul Ţării Moldovei, p. 133–134.

[13] Brezeanu, Stelian (1999). *Romanitatea Orientală în Evul Mediu*. Bucharest: Editura All Educational. pp. 229–246.

[14] In his well known literary testament Ienăchiţă Văcărescu writes: "Urmaşilor mei Văcăreşti!/Las vouă moştenire:/Creşterea limbei româneşti/Ş-a patriei cinstire."

In the *"Istoria faptelor lui Mavroghene-Vodă şi a răzmeriţei din timpul lui pe la 1790"* a Pitar Hristache writes: "Încep după-a mea ideie/Cu vreo câteva condeie/Povestea mavroghenească/Dela Ţara Românească.

[15] The first known mention of the term "Romania" in its modern denotation dates from 1816, as the Greek scholar Dimitrie Daniel Philippide published in Leipzig his work "The History of Romania", followed by "The Geography of Romania".

On the tombstone of Gheorghe Lazăr in Avrig (built in 1823) there is the inscription: "Precum Hristos pe Lazăr din morţi a înviat/Aşa tu România din somn ai deşteptat."

[16] " Wallachia and Moldavia, 1859-61 (http://www.fotw.net/flags/ro-wm.html)". . Retrieved 2008-01-05.

[17] " Map of Southern Europe, 1942-1945 (http://www.lib.utexas.edu/maps/historical/s_approaches_1942-1945.jpg)". United States Army Center of Military History via the University of Texas at Austin Perry-Castañeda Library Map Collection. . Retrieved 2008-08-31.

[18] " General principles (http://www.cdep.ro/pls/dic/site.page?den=act2_2&par1=1#t1c0s0a1)" (in Romanian). cdep.ro. . Retrieved 2009-09-07.

[19] Trinkaus, E. (2003). "Early Modern Human Cranial remains from the Peştera cu Oase". *Journal of Human Evolution* **45**: 245–253. doi: 10.1016/j.jhevol.2003.08.003 (http://dx.doi.org/10.1016/j.jhevol.2003.08.003).

[20] Zilhão, João (2006). "Neanderthals and Moderns Mixed and It Matters". *Evolutionary Anthropology* **15**: 183–195. doi: 10.1002/evan.20110 (http://dx.doi.org/10.1002/evan.20110).

[21] Herodotus (1859). *The Ancient History of Herodotus By Herodotus* (http://books.google.com/books?id=sfHsgNIZum0C&pg=PA215& lpg=PA215&dq=herodotus+dacians+darius&source=web&ots=G4uX7Mnsqb&sig=kYPtXH157JEzuk7V618EreDadqY&hl=en). Derby & Jackson. pp. 213–217. . Retrieved 2008-01-10.

[22] " Assorted Imperial Battle Descriptions (http://www.roman-emperors.org/assobd.htm#s-inx)". De Imperatoribus Romanis, An Online Encyclopedia of Roman Emperors. . Retrieved 2008-01-10.

[23] " Dacia-Province of the Roman Empire (http://www.unrv.com/provinces/dacia.php)". United Nations of Roma Victor. . Retrieved 2008-01-10.

[24] Deletant, Dennis (1995). *Colloquial Romanian*. New York: Routledge. pp. 1. ISBN 9780415129008.

[25] Matley, Ian (1970). *Romania; a Profile*. Praeger. pp. 85.

[26] Giurescu, Constantin C. (1972). *The Making of the Romanian People and Language*. Bucharest: Meridiane Publishing House. pp. 43, 98–101,141.

[27] Eutropius; Justin, Cornelius Nepos (1886). *Eutropius, Abridgment of Roman History* (http://www.ccel.org/p/pearse/morefathers/eutropius_breviarium_2_text.htm). London: George Bell and Sons. . Retrieved 2008-08-31.

[28] Watkins, Thayer. " The Economic History of the Western Roman Empire (http://www.sjsu.edu/faculty/watkins/barbarians.htm)". . Retrieved 2008-08-31. ""The Emperor Aurelian recognized the realities of the military situation in Dacia and around 271 A.D. withdrew Roman troops from Dacia leaving it to the Goths. The Danube once again became the northern frontier of the Roman Empire in eastern Europe""

[29] Ghyka, Matila (1841). " A Documented Chronology of Roumanian History (http://web.archive.org/web/20070125091613/http://www.vlachophiles.net/ghika.htm)" B. H. Blackwell Ltd.. Archived from the original (http://www.vlachophiles.net/ghika.htm) on 2007-01-25. . Retrieved 2008-08-31.

[30] Jordanes (551 A.D.). *Getica, sive, De Origine Actibusque Gothorum* (http://www.harbornet.com/folks/theedrich/Goths/Goths1.htm). Constantinople. . Retrieved 2008-08-31.

[31] Iliescu, Vl.; Paschale, Chronicon (1970). *Fontes Historiae Daco-Romanae*. **II**. Bucureşti. pp. 363, 587.

[32] Teodor, Dan Gh. (1995). *Istoria României de la începuturi până în secolul al VIII-lea*. 2. Bucureşti. pp. 294–325.

[33] Bona, Istvan (2001). " History of Transylvania: II.3. The Kingdom of the Gepids (http://mek.oszk.hu/03400/03407/html/33.html)". in Köpeczi, Bela. Institute of History of the Hungarian Academy of Sciences. . Retrieved 2008-08-31.

[34] Bona, Istvan (2001). " History of Transylvania: II.4. The Period of the Avar Rule (http://mek.oszk.hu/03400/03407/html/41.html)". in Köpeczi, Bela. Institute of History of the Hungarian Academy of Sciences. . Retrieved 2008-08-31.

[35] Constantine VII, Porphyrogenitus (950). *Constantine Porphyrogenitus De Administrando Imperio* (http://faculty.washington.edu/dwaugh/rus/texts/constp.html). Constantinople. . Retrieved 2008-08-31.

[36] Xenopol, Alexandru D. (1896). *Histoire des Roumains*. Paris. pp. 168.

[37] Makkai, Laszlo (2001). " History of Transylvania: III. Transylvania in the Medieval Hungarian Kingdom (896–1526) (http://mek.oszk.hu/03400/03407/html/57.html)". in Köpeczi, Bela. Institute of History of the Hungarian Academy of Sciences. . Retrieved 2008-08-31.

[38] Köpeczi, Bela, ed (2001). " History of Transylvania: IV. The First Period of the Principality of Transylvania (1526–1606) (http://mek.oszk.hu/03400/03407/html/97.html)". Institute of History of the Hungarian Academy of Sciences. . Retrieved 2008-08-31.

[39] Varkonyi, Agnes R. (2001). Köpeczi, Bela. ed *History of Transylvania: VI. The Last Decades of the Independent Principality (1660–1711)* (http://mek.oszk.hu/03400/03407/html/221.html). 2. New York: Institute of History of the Hungarian Academy of Sciences. . Retrieved 2008-08-31.

[40] Ştefănescu, Ştefan (1991). *Istoria medie a României*. I. Bucharest. pp. 114.

[41] Predescu, Lucian (1940). "Enciclopedia Cugetarea". *Enciclopedia Cugetarea*.

[42] Vlad III (ruler of Walachia) (http://www.britannica.com/EBchecked/topic/631524/Vlad-III). Britannica Online Encyclopedia.

[43] Istvan, Vasary. " Cumans and Tatars (http://www.cambridge.org/catalogue/catalogue.asp?isbn=9780511110153&ss=fro)". cambridge.org. . Retrieved 2009-09-07.

[44] Rezachevici, Constantin (2000). " Mihai Viteazul: itinerariul moldovean (http://www.itcnet.ro/history/archive/mi2000/current5/mi5.htm)" (in Romanian). *Magazin istoric* (5). . Retrieved 2008-08-31.

[45] " The Magyarization Process (http://www.genealogy.ro/cont/13.htm)". GenealogyRO Group. . Retrieved 2008-08-31.

[46] Kocsis, Karoly; Kocsis-Hodosi, Eszter (1999). *Ethnic structure of the population on the present territory of Transylvania (1880-1992)* (http://www.hungarian-history.hu/lib/hmcb/Tab14.htm). . Retrieved 2008-08-31.

[47] Kocsis, Karoly; Kocsis-Hodosi, Eszter (2001). *Ethnic Geography of the Hungarian Minorities in the Carpathian Basin*. Simon Publications. pp. 102. ISBN 193131375X.

[48] Prodan, David (1971). *Supplex Libellus Valachorum= Or, The Politicle Struggle of Romanians in Transylvania During the 18th Century*. Bucharest: Academy of Social Republic of Romania.

[49] Bobango, Gerald J (1979). *The emergence of the Romanian national State*. New York: Boulder. ISBN 9780914710516.

[50] " San Stefano Preliminary Treaty (http://www.hist.msu.ru/ER/Etext/FOREIGN/stefano.htm)". 1878. . Retrieved 2008-08-31.

[51] *The Treaty of Berlin, 1878 - Excerpts on the Balkans* (http://www.fordham.edu/halsall/mod/1878berlin.html). Berlin: Fordham University. July 13, 1878. . Retrieved 2008-08-31.

[52] Patterson, Michelle (August 1996). " The Road to Romanian Independence (http://findarticles.com/p/articles/mi_qa3686/is_199608/ai_n8755098)" (WP:Dead external links – Scholar search (http://scholar.google.co.uk/scholar?hl=en&lr=&q=author:Patterson+intitle:The+Road+to+Romanian+Independence&as_publication=Canadian+Journal+of+History&as_ylo=1996&as_yhi=1996&btnG=Search)).

Canadian Journal of History. . Retrieved 2008-08-31.

[53] Anderson, Frank Maloy; Hershey, Amos Shartle (1918). *Handbook for the Diplomatic History of Europe, Asia, and Africa 1870-1914*. Washington D.C.: Government Printing Office.

[54] Horne, Charles F. (Horne). " Ion Bratianu's Declaration of War Delivered to the Austrian Minister in Romania on August 28, 1916 (http://www.firstworldwar.com/source/romaniawardeclaration.htm)". Source Records of the Great War. . Retrieved 2008-08-31.

[55] Erlikman, Vadim (2004). *Poteri narodonaseleniia v XX veke : spravochnik*. Moscow. ISBN 5-93165-107-1.

[56] " Text of the Treaty of Trianon (http://wwi.lib.byu.edu/index.php/Treaty_of_Trianon)". World War I Document Archive. . Retrieved 2008-08-31.

[57] Bernard Anthony Cook (2001). *Europe Since 1945: An Encyclopedia*. Taylor&Francis. p. 162. ISBN 0815340575.

[58] Malbone W. Graham (October 1944). " The Legal Status of the Bukovina and Bessarabia (http://www.jstor.org/stable/2192802)". *The American Journal of International Law* (American Society of International Law) **38** (4). . Retrieved 2008-08-31.

[59] " Statul National Unitar (România Mare 1919 - 1940)publisher=ici.ro (http://media.ici.ro/history/ist08.htm)" (in Romanian). . Retrieved 2008-08-31.

[60] Ioan Scurtu, Theodora Stănescu-Stanciu, Georgiana Margareta Scurtu (2002) (in Romanian). *Istoria Românilor între anii 1918-1940* (http://www.unibuc.ro/eBooks/istorie/istorie1918-1940/13-4.htm). University of Bucharest. .

[61] Nagy-Talavera, Nicolas M. (1970). *Green Shirts and Others: a History of Fascism in Hungary and Romania*. Hoover Institution Press. p. 305.

[62] M. Broszat (1968). "Deutschland — Ungarn — Rumänien. Entwicklung und Grundfaktoren nationalsozialistischer Hegemonial- und Bündnispolitik 1938-1941" (in German). *Historische Zeitschrift* (206): 552–553.

[63] " The Biggest Mistakes In World War 2:Ploesti - the most important target (http://www.2worldwar2.com/mistakes.htm#ploesti)". . Retrieved 2008-08-31.

[64] *Note: follow the World War II link*: (2005-11-09) *Romania:World War II* (http://lcweb2.loc.gov/frd/cs/rotoc.html), Washington D.C.: Library of Congress.Federal Research Division. Report. Retrieved on 2008-08-31.

[65] Raul Hilberg; Yad Vashem (2004). " Executive Summary: Historical Findings and Recommendations (http://yad-vashem.org.il/about_yad/what_new/data_whats_new/pdf/english/EXECUTIVE_SUMMARY.pdf)" (PDF). International Commission on the Holocaust in Romania. . Retrieved 2008-08-31. ""no country, besides Germany, was involved in massacres of Jews on such a scale.""

[66] Eugen Tomiuc (May 6, 2005). " World War II – 60 Years After: Former Romanian Monarch Remembers Decision To Switch Sides (http://web.archive.org/web/20070930033400/http://www.rferl.org/featuresarticle/2005/5/38D4D252-BE7E-4943-A6A9-4E3C1B32A05F.html)". Archived from the original (http://www.rferl.org/featuresarticle/2005/5/38D4D252-BE7E-4943-A6A9-4E3C1B32A05F.html) on 2007-09-30. . Retrieved 2008-08-31.

[67] Michael Clodfelter (2002). *Warfare and Armed Conflicts- A Statistical Reference to Casualty and Other Figures, 1500-2000* (2 ed.). Jefferson, NC: McFarland. pp. 582. ISBN 0-7864-1204-6.

[68] Martin Gilbert. *Atlas of the Holocaust.* 1988

[69] " Romania: Country studies - Chapter 1.7.1 "Petru Groza's Premiership" (http://lcweb2.loc.gov/frd/cs/rotoc.html#ro0037)". Federal research Division, Library of Congress. . Retrieved 2008-08-31.

[70] " Romania (https://www.cia.gov/library/publications/the-world-factbook/geos/ro.html)". CIA - The World Factbook. . Retrieved 2008-08-31.

[71] " Romania - Country Background and Profile (http://www.ed-u.com/ro.html)". ed-u.com. . Retrieved 2008-08-31.

[72] Rîjnoveanu, Carmen (2003). " Romania's Policy of Autonomy in the Context of the Sino-Soviet Conflict (http://www.servicehistorique.sga.defense.gouv.fr/07autredossiers/groupetravailhistoiremilitaire/pdfs/2003-gthm.pdf)" (PDF). Czech Republic Military History Institute, Militärgeschichtliches Forscheungamt. pp. 1. . Retrieved 2008-08-31.

[73] Roper, Stephen D. (2000). *Romania: The Unfinished Revolution*. London: Routledge. pp. 18. ISBN 9058230279.

[74] Cioroianu, Adrian (2005) (in Romanian). *"On the Shoulders of Marx. An Incursion into the History of Romanian Communism"*. Bucharest: Editura Curtea Veche. pp. 68–73. ISBN 9736691756.

[75] Caraza, Grigore (2004) (in Romanian). *Aiud însângerat*. **Chapter IV**. Editura Vremea XXI. ISBN 9736450503.Wikipedia:Citing sources

[76] Cicerone Ioniţoiu (2000) (in Romanian). *Victimele terorii comuniste. Arestaţi, torturaţi, întemniţaţi, ucişi. Dicţionar*. Bucharest: Editura Maşina de scris. ISBN 973-99994-2-5.Wikipedia:Citing sources

[77] " Romania: Soviet Union and Eastern Europe (http://countrystudies.us/romania/75.htm)". Country Studies.us. . Retrieved 2008-08-31.

[78] " Middle East policies in Communist Romania (http://countrystudies.us/romania/80.htm)". Country Studies.us. . Retrieved 2008-08-31.

[79] Deletant, Dennis. " New Evidence on Romania and the Warsaw Pact, 1955-1989 (http://www.wilsoncenter.org/index.cfm?topic_id=1409&fuseaction=topics.publications&doc_id=16367&group_id=13349)". Cold War International History Project e-Dossier Series. . Retrieved 2008-08-31.

[80] (2004) *Recensământul populaţiei concentraţionare din România în anii 1945-1989*. Sighet: Centrul Internaţional de Studii asupra Comunismului. Report.

[81] (2006-12-15) *Raportul Comisiei Prezidenţiale pentru Analiza Dictaturii Comuniste din România*. Comisia Prezidenţială pentru Analiza Dictaturii Comuniste din România, 215–217. Report.

[82] Carothers, Thomas. " Romania: The Political Background (http://www.idea.int/publications/country/upload/Romania, The Political Background.pdf)" (PDF). . Retrieved 2008-08-31. ""This seven-year period can be characterized as a gradualistic, often ambiguous transition away from communist rule towards democracy.""

[83] Hellman, Joel (January 1998). "Winners Take All: The Politics of Partial Reform in Postcommunist". *Transitions World Politics* **50** (2): 203–234.

[84] Bohlen, Celestine. " Evolution in Europe; Romanian miners invade Bucharest (http://query.nytimes.com/gst/fullpage. html?res=9C0CE6D6113DF936A25755C0A966958260)". . Retrieved 2008-08-31.

[85] " NATO update: NATO welcomes seven new members (http://www.nato.int/docu/update/2004/04-april/e0402a.htm)". NATO. . Retrieved 2008-08-31.

[86] " EU approves Bulgaria and Romania (http://news.bbc.co.uk/1/hi/world/europe/5380024.stm)". BBC News. . Retrieved 2008-08-31.

[87] " Romania (http://www.focus-migration.de/index.php?id=2515&L=1)". focus-migration.de. . Retrieved 2008-08-28.

[88] " Geography, Meteorology and Environment (http://www.insse.ro/cms/files/pdf/ro/cap1.pdf)" (in Romanian). Romanian Statistical Yearbook. 2004. . Retrieved 2009-09-07.

[89] " Danube Delta (http://whc.unesco.org/en/list/588)". UNESCO's World Heritage Center. . Retrieved 2008-01-09.

[90] " Romania's Biodiversity (http://enrin.grida.no/biodiv/biodiv/national/romania/robiodiv.htm)". Ministry of Waters, Forests and Environmental Protection of Romania. . Retrieved 2008-01-10.

[91] " State of the Environment in Romania 1998: Biodiversity (http://www.envir.ee/programmid/pharecd/soes/romania/html/biodiversity/ index.htm)". Romanian Ministry of Waters, Forests and Environmental Protection. . Retrieved 2008-01-10.

[92] " EarthTrends:Biodiversity and Protected Areas - Romania (http://earthtrends.wri.org/pdf_library/country_profiles/bio_cou_642.pdf)" (PDF). . Retrieved 2008-01-10.

[93] " Protected Areas in Romania (http://www.envir.ee/programmid/pharecd/soes/romania/html/biodiversity/ariiprot/protarea.htm)". Romanian Ministry of Waters, Forests and Environmental Protection. . Retrieved 2008-01-10.

[94] " Danube Delta Reserve Biosphere (http://www.envir.ee/programmid/pharecd/soes/romania/html/biodiversity/ariiprot/delta.htm)". Romanian Ministry of Waters, Forests and Environmental Protection. . Retrieved 2008-01-10.

[95] " Danube Delta (http://whc.unesco.org/en/list/588)". UNESCO's World Heritage Center. . Retrieved 2008-01-10.

[96] " NHK World Heritage 100 Series (http://whc.unesco.org/en/list/588/video)". UNESCO's World Heritage Center. . Retrieved 2008-01-10.

[97] " Flora si fauna salbatica (http://enrin.grida.no/htmls/romania/soe2000/rom/cap5/ff.htm)" (in Romanian). enrin.grida.no. . Retrieved 2009-09-07.

[98] " Capitolul 12: Relief, apele, clima, vegetatia, fauna, ariile protejate (http://www.rri.ro/art.shtml?lang=2&sec=252&art=18152)" (in Romanian). *Aproape totul despre România*. Radio Romania International. . Retrieved 2009-09-07.

[99] " Land   Plant and animal life (http://www.britannica.com/EBchecked/topic/508461/Romania)". Encyclopædia Britannica. . Retrieved 2009-09-07.

[100] " Romania: Climate (http://countrystudies.us/romania/34.htm)". U.S. Library of Congress. . Retrieved 2008-01-10.

[101] " Romania: climate (http://www.romaniatourism.com/climate.html)". Climate. . Retrieved 2008-01-10.

[102] " The monthly average climate parameters in Bucharest (http://www.wordtravels.com/Travelguide/Countries/Romania/Climate/)". WorldTravels. . Retrieved 2008-01-10.

[103] " Permafrost Monitoring and Prediction in Southern Carpathians, Romania (http://clic.npolar.no/disc/disc_datasets_metadata. php?s=0&desc=1&table=Datasets&id=DISC_GCMD_GGD30&tag=All&Category=&WCRP=&Location=All&stype=phrase& limit=10&q=)". CliC International Project Office (CIPO). 2004-12-22. . Retrieved 2008-08-31.

[104] " The 2004 Yearbook (http://www.insse.ro/cms/files/pdf/ro/cap1.pdf)" (in Romanian) (PDF). Romanian National Institute of Statistics. . Retrieved 2008-08-31.

[105] 2002 census data, based on Population by ethnicity (http://www.recensamant.ro/pagini/tabele/t47.pdf), gives a total of 535,250 Roma in Romania. This figure is disputed by other sources, because at the local level, many Roma declare a different ethnicity (mostly Romanian, but also Hungarian in the West and Turkish in Dobruja) for fear of discrimination. Many are not recorded at all, since they do not have ID cards (http://www.edrc.ro/docs/docs/Romii_din_Romania.pdf). International sources give higher figures than the official census(UNDP's Regional Bureau for Europe (http://europeandcis.undp.org/uploads/public/File/rbec_web/vgr/chapter1.1.pdf), World Bank (http:// web.worldbank.org/WBSITE/EXTERNAL/COUNTRIES/ECAEXT/EXTROMA/ 0,,contentMDK:20333806~menuPK:615999~pagePK:64168445~piPK:64168309~theSitePK:615987,00.html), " International Association for Official Statistics (http://web.archive.org/web/20080226202154/http://www.msd.govt.nz/documents/publications/msd/journal/ issue25/25-pages154-164.pdf)" (PDF). Archived from the original (http://www.msd.govt.nz/documents/publications/msd/journal/ issue25/25-pages154-164.pdf) on 2008-02-26. ..

[106] " European effort spotlights plight of the Roma (http://www.usatoday.com/news/world/2005-02-01-roma-europe_x.htm)". usatoday. . Retrieved 2008-08-31.

[107] *Official site of the results of the 2002 Census* (http://www.recensamant.ro/pagini/rezultate.html). Report. Retrieved on 2008-08-31.

[108] " German Population of Romania, 1930-1948 (http://www.hungarian-history.hu/lib/minor/min02.htm)". hungarian-history.hu. . Retrieved 2009-09-07.

[109] " German minority (http://www.auswaertiges-amt.de/diplo/en/Laenderinformationen/01-Laender/Rumaenien.html)". auswaertiges-amt.de. . Retrieved 2009-09-07.

[110] " The Virtual Jewish History Tour - Romania (http://www.jewishvirtuallibrary.org/jsource/vjw/romania.html)". jewishvirtuallibrary.org. . Retrieved 2009-09-07.

[111] " Outsourcing IT în România (http://www.anis.ro/index.php?page=afaceri&sec=afaceri_avantaje&lang=ro)" (in Romanian). Owners Association of the Software and Service Industry. . Retrieved 2008-08-31.

[112] " Chronology of the International Organization La Francophonie (http://www.francophonie.org/doc/doc-historique/chronologie-oif. pdf)" (in French) (pfd). . Retrieved 2008-08-31.

[113] *Romanian Census Website with population by religion* (http://www.recensamant.ro/datepr/tbl6.html). Recensamant.ro. Report. Retrieved on 2008-01-01.

[114] " Romania President Approves Europe's "Worst Religion Law" (http://www.bosnewslife.com/europe/romania/ 2674-romania-president-approves-europes-worst/)". . Retrieved 2008-08-31.

[115] " Population of the largest cities and towns in Romania (http://www.world-gazetteer.com/wg.php?x=1186654811&men=gcis& lng=en&des=gamelan&dat=200&geo=-182&srt=pnan&col=aohdqcfbeimg&pt=c&va=&srt=1pnan)". World Gazetteer. . Retrieved 2008-08-31.

[116] " Metropolitan Zone of Bucharest will be ready in 10 years (http://www.romanialibera.ro/a94321/ zona-metropolitana-bucuresti-va-fi-gata-peste-10-ani.html)" (in Romanian). *Romania Libera*. . Retrieved 2008-08-31.

[117] " Official site of Metropolitan Zone of Bucharest Project (http://www.zmb.ro/main.php)" (in Romanian). . Retrieved 2008-08-31.

[118] " Map of Romanian municipalities that can have metorpolitan areas in maroon (http://www.zmi.ro/de/zmi_context_romania.html)". . Retrieved 2008-08-31.

[119] *The Romanian Educational Policy in Transition* (http://www.unesco.org/education/wef/countryreports/romania/rapport_1.html). UNESCO. Report. Retrieved on 2008-08-31.

[120] *The Romanian Educational Policy in Transition* (http://www.unesco.org/education/wef/countryreports/romania/rapport_2.html). UNESCO. Report. Retrieved on 2008-08-31.

[121] " Limited relevants. What feminists can learn from the eastern experience (http://www.genderomania.ro/book_gender_post/part1/ Anca_Gheaus.pdf)" (pdf). genderomania.ro. . Retrieved 2008-08-25.

[122] " Romanian Institute of Statistics Yearbook - Chapter 8 (http://www.insse.ro/cms/files/pdf/ro/cap8.pdf)" (in Romanian) (PDF). . Retrieved 2008-08-31.

[123] " UN Human Development Report 2006 (http://web.archive.org/web/20070202212856/http://hdr.undp.org/hdr2006/pdfs/report/ HDR06-complete.pdf)" (pdf). Archived from the original (http://hdr.undp.org/hdr2006/pdfs/report/HDR06-complete.pdf) on 2007-02-02. .

[124] (2002) *OECD International Program for Evaluation of Students, National Report* (http://www.edu.ro/index.php?module=uploads& func=download&fileId=1958). București: Romanian Ministry of Education, 10—15. Report. Retrieved on 2008-08-31.

[125] *Academic Ranking World University 2006: Top 500 World University* (http://ed.sjtu.edu.cn/rank/2006/ARWU2006FULLLIST-BY RANK (PDF).pdf). Report. Retrieved on 2008-08-31.

[126] Răzvan Florian *Romanian Universities and the Shanghai rankings* (http://www.ad-astra.ro/journal/8/florian_shanghai_romania.pdf), Cluj-Napoca, România: Asociația Ad Astra a cercetătorilor rom âni, 7–9. Report. Retrieved on 2008-08-31.

[127] " Romania removes theory of evolution from school curriculum (http://www.thediplomat.ro/reports_1207.php)". *The Diplomat*. . Retrieved 2008-08-31.

[128] *Romania*. 2 (48 ed.). London and New York: Routledge. 2007. pp. 3734–3759. ISBN 9781857434125.

[129] " Presentation (http://www.scj.ro/monogr_en.asp)". High Court of Cassation and Justice - —Romania. . Retrieved 2008-08-31.

[130] " Romanian Legal system (http://permanent.access.gpo.gov/lps35389/2000//legal_system.html)". CIA Factbook. 2000. . Retrieved 2008-01-11.

[131] Bos, Stefan (01 January 2007). " Bulgaria, Romania Join European Union (http://voanews.com/english/archive/2007-01/ 2007-01-01-voa16.cfm)". *VOA News* (Voice of America). . Retrieved 2 January 2009.

[132] " Romania will be EU's most corrupt new member (http://www.bbj.hu/main/news_18741_romania+will+be+eus+most+corrupt+ new+member.html)". . Retrieved 2008-01-11.

[133] " Geografia Romaniei (http://www.descopera.net/romania_geografie.html)" (in Romanian). descopera.net. . Retrieved 2009-09-07.

[134] *Administrative Organisation of Romanian Territory, on December 31, 2005* (http://www.insse.ro/cms/files/pdf/ro/cap1.pdf), Romanian National Institute of Statistics. Report. Retrieved on 2008-08-31.

[135] " Hierarchical list of the Nomenclature of territorial units for statistics - NUTS and the Statistical regions of Europe (http://web.archive. org/web/20080118234301/http://ec.europa.eu/comm/eurostat/ramon/nuts/codelist_en.cfm?list=nuts)". Archived from the original (http://ec.europa.eu/comm/eurostat/ramon/nuts/codelist_en.cfm?list=nuts) on 2008-01-18. . Retrieved 2008-08-31.

[136] " Foreign Policy Priorities of Romania for 2008 (http://www.mae.ro/index.php?unde=doc&id=35181&idlnk=1&cat=3)" (in Romanian). Romanian Ministry of Foreign Affairs. . Retrieved 2008-08-28.

[137] " Turkey & Romania hand in hand for a better tomorrow. (http://www.thenewanatolian.com/ek6.pdf)" (PDF). The New Anatolian, February 1, 2006. .

[138] Government of Romania (2006-03-24). " Headline: Meeting with the Hungarian Prime Minister, Ferenc Gyurcsany (http://www.guv.ro/ engleza/presa/afis-doc.php?idpresa=6372&idrubricapresa=&idrubricaprimm=&idtema=&tip=&pag=&dr=)". Press release. . Retrieved 2008-08-31.

[139] " Background Note: Romania - U.S.-Romanian Relations (http://www.state.gov/r/pa/ei/bgn/35722.htm)". U.S. Department of State. .

[140] http://www.bucharestherald.com/politics/34-politics/ 3116-hillary-clinton-romania-one-of-the-most-trustworthy-and-respectable-partners-of-the-usa-

[141] Gabriel Andreescu, Valentin Stan, Renate Weber (1994-10-30). " Romania'S Relations With The Republic Of Moldova (http://studint. ong.ro/moldova.htm)". *International Studies* (Center for International Studies). . Retrieved 2008-08-31.

[142] Stefan Ihrig. " Rediscovering History, Rediscovering Ultimate Truth (http://www.desk.c.u-tokyo.ac.jp/download/es_5_Ihrig.pdf)" (PDF). . Retrieved 2008-09-17.

[143] "Moldova urging Romania to sign basic political treaty". Romania News Watch. 2007-12-16.

[144] Ministry of National Defense of Romania (2003-01-21). " Press conference (http://www.mapn.ro/briefing/030122/030121conf.htm)". Press release. . Retrieved 2008-08-31.

[145] " MoND Budget as of 2007 (http://www.zf.ro/articol_99920/bugetul_mapn__2_05__din_pib__in_2007.html)" (in Romanian). *Ziarul Financiar*. 2006-10-30. . Retrieved 2008-08-31.

[146] " SUA şi UE se intrec să ne doboare MiG-urile (http://www.cotidianul.ro/index.php?id=45&art=25285&nr=3&cHash=b2e1d334a5)". *Cotidianul*. January 2007. . Retrieved 2008-08-31.

[147] "Spartan Order". *Aviation Week & Space Technology*. 2006-12-11.

[148] " IMF World Economic Outlook April 2008 - Central and Eastern Europe (http://www.imf.org/external/pubs/ft/weo/2008/01/ weodata/weorept.aspx?sy=2006&ey=2013&scsm=1&ssd=1&sort=country&ds=.&br=1&c=968& s=NGDP_RPCH,NGDPD,NGDPDPC,PPPGDP,PPPPC,PCPIPCH&grp=0&a=&pr1.x=87&pr1.y=12)". IMF. April 2008. . Retrieved 2008-08-31.

[149] " Country Classification Groups (http://web.worldbank.org/WBSITE/EXTERNAL/DATASTATISTICS/ 0,,contentMDK:20421402~pagePK:64133150~piPK:64133175~theSitePK:239419,00.html#Upper_middle_income)". World Bank. 2005. . Retrieved 2008-08-31.

[150] " GDP in 2006 (http://www.insse.ro/cms/files/statistici/comunicate/pib/pibr06.pdf)" (in Romanian) (PDF). Romanian National Institute of Statistics. . Retrieved 2008-01-10.

[151] " World Bank: In 2008 Romania will have an economic growth of 5.9% (http://www.romanialibera.ro/a115093/ banca-mondiala-in-2008-romania-va-avea-o-crestere-economica-de-5-9.html)" (in Romanian). . Retrieved 2008-01-13.

[152] " Creşterea economică din 2008 a frânat brusc în T 4 (http://www.curierulnational.ro/Economie/2009-03-05/Cresterea+economica+ din+2008+a+franat+brusc+in+T+4)" (in Romanian). *Curierul National*. . Retrieved 2009-09-07.

[153] " GDP per capita in PPS (http://epp.eurostat.ec.europa.eu/cache/ITY_PUBLIC/2-25062009-BP/EN/2-25062009-BP-EN.PDF)". Eurostat. . Retrieved 2009-06-25.

[154] " Main Macroeconomic Indicators, September 2007 (http://www.insse.ro/cms/files/statistici/comunicate/lunar_indicatori/a07/ sic09r07.pdf)" (in Romanian) (PDF). National Institute of Statistics of Romania. . Retrieved 2008-08-31.

[155] " Romania (https://www.cia.gov/library/publications/the-world-factbook/geos/ro.html)". CIA World Factbook. 2006. . Retrieved 2008-08-31.

[156] " Romania at A Glance - January 2008 (http://romaniaeconomywatch.blogspot.com/2007/11/romania-trade-balance-september 2007. html)". Romania Economy Watch. January 2008. . Retrieved 2008-01-10.

[157] " Index of Economic Freedom: Romania (http://www.heritage.org/research/features/index/country.cfm?id=Romania)". heritage.org. . Retrieved 2008-08-31.

[158] (2007-06-26) *Taxation trends in the EU* (http://epp.eurostat.ec.europa.eu/pls/portal/docs/PAGE/PGP_PRD_CAT_PREREL/ PGE_CAT_PREREL_YEAR_2007/PGE_CAT_PREREL_YEAR_2007_MONTH_06/2-26062007-EN-AP.PDF), Eurostat. Report. Retrieved on 2008-08-31.

[159] " Romania: FDI reached over EUR 8.3 bn (http://www.portalino.it/nuke/modules.php?name=News&file=article&sid=20346)". . Retrieved 2008-08-31.

[160] (2007) *Economy Ranking* (http://www.doingbusiness.org/EconomyRankings/). World Bank. Report. Retrieved on 2008-08-31.

[161] *Doing Business 2007 Report* (http://web.worldbank.org/WBSITE/EXTERNAL/NEWS/ 0,,contentMDK:21041782~pagePK:64257043~piPK:437376~theSitePK:4607,00.html). World Bank. Report. Retrieved on 2008-08-31.

[162] *Average wage in May 2009* (http://www.insse.ro/cms/files/statistici/comunicate/castiguri/a09/cs05r09.pdf), National Institute of Statistics, Romania. Report. Retrieved on 2009-07-28.

[163] " Implied PPP conversion rate for Romania (http://www.imf.org/external/pubs/ft/weo/2008/01/weodata/weorept.aspx?x=30& pr.y=8&sy=2006&ey=2013&scsm=1&ssd=1&sort=country&ds=.&br=1&c=968&s=PPPEX&grp=0&a=)". IMF. April 2008. . Retrieved 2008-08-31.

[164] " Prezentarea generală a reţelei de drumuri (http://www.cnadnr.ro/pagina.php?idg=20)" (in Romanian). cnadnr.ro. . Retrieved 2009-09-07.

[165] " Reteaua feroviara (http://www.cfr.ro/jf/romana/0208/retea.htm)" (in Romanian). cfr.to. . Retrieved 2009-09-06.

[166] " Metrorex ridership (http://www.sfin.ro/articol_8634/transferul_metrorex_la_primaria_capitalei_a_incins_spiritele.html)" (in Romanian). Financial Week newspaper. April 23, 2007. . Retrieved 2008-08-31.

[167] " Country/Economy Profiles: Romania, Travel&Tourism (http://www.weforum.org/pdf/tourism/Romania.pdf)" (PDF). World Economic Forum. . Retrieved 2008-01-11.

[168] " WTTC spells out policy recommendations for Romania to tap travel and tourism potential (http://www.wttc.travel/eng/ News_and_Events/Press/Press_Releases_2006/WTTC_spells_out_recommendations_for_Romania/index.php)". WTTC. . Retrieved 2008-01-11.

[169] " 20 million overnight stays by international tourists (http://aktirom.com/index.php?option=com_content&task=view&id=2& Itemid=2)". . Retrieved 2008-01-11.

[170] *Report from Romanian National Institute of Statistics* (http://www.insse.ro/cms/files/statistici/comunicate/turism/a07/turism09e07. pdf). Report. Retrieved on 2008-01-11. "for the first 9 months of 2007 an increase from the previous year of 8.7% to 16.5 million tourists; of these 94.0% came from European countries and 61.7% from EU"

[171] " Tourism attracted in 2005 investments worth €400 million (http://www.gandul.info/social/ turismul-atras-2005-investitii-400-milioane-euro.html?3932;255059)" (in ro). *Gandul* Newspaper. . Retrieved 2008-01-11.

[172] " Tan and fun at the Black Sea (http://www.unseenromania.com/places-to-go-romania/tan-and-fun-at-the-black-sea.html)". UnseenRomania. . Retrieved 2008-01-10.

[173] " Turismul renaste la tara (http://www.romanialibera.ro/a128995/turismul-renaste-la-tara.html)" (in Romanian). Romania Libera. 2008-07-05. . Retrieved 2008-08-28.

[174] " Bine ati venit pe site-ul de promovare a pensiunilor agroturistice din Romania !!! (http://www.ruraltourism.ro/)" (in Romanian). RuralTourism.ro. . Retrieved 2008-08-28.

[175] " Romania - Culture (http://www.itcnet.ro/folk_festival/culture.htm)". . Retrieved 2008-08-31.

[176] Lucian Boia, James Christian Brown (2001). *Romania: Borderland of Europe*. Reaktion Books. pp. 13, 36–40. ISBN 9781861891037.

[177] " Cultural aspects (http://www.ici.ro/romania/en/cultura/cultural_aspects.html)". National Institute for Research & Development in Informatics, Romania. . Retrieved 2008-08-28.

[178] Luis Bush. " Romania Prepares for GCOWE September 20, 1994 (http://www.missionfrontiers.org/1994/1112/nd9416.htm)". Mission Frontiers. . Retrieved 2008-08-31.

[179] " Mihai Eminescu (http://www.ici.ro/romania/en/cultura/l_eminescu.html)" (in Romanian). National Institute for Research & Development in Informatics, Romania. . Retrieved 2008-01-20.

[180] Mona Momescu. " Romanian Cultural Debate of the Summer: Romanian Intellectuals and Their Status Groups (http://www.columbia. edu/cu/romanian/articles/TheRomanianCulturalDebateOfTheSummer.html)". Romanian Club @ Columbia University. . Retrieved 2008-08-28.

[181] " Constantin Brâncuşi's bio (http://www.brancusi.com/bio.html)". Brancusi.com. . Retrieved 2008-01-20.

[182] " Brancusi's 'Bird in Space' Sets World Auction Record for Sculpture at $27,456,000 (http://antiquesandthearts.com/ AW-2005-05-10-12-15-39p1.htm)". Antiques and the Arts Online. . Retrieved 2008-01-20.

[183] " November 9, The price record for a Brancusi masterpiece was set up in 2005 when "Bird in Space" was sold for USD 27.5 M (http:// crib.mae.ro/index.php?lang=en&id=31&s=15441&arhiva=true)". Romanian Information Center in Brussels. . Retrieved 2008-01-20.

[184] " George Enescu, the composer (http://www.enescusociety.org/georgeenescu.php)". International Enescu Society. . Retrieved 2008-01-20.

[185] " George Enescu (1881 - 1955) (http://www.ici.ro/romania/en/cultura/m_enescu.html)". National Institute for Research & Development in Informatics, Romania. . Retrieved 2008-01-20.

[186] Ştefănescu, Alex. (1999) (in Romanian). *Nichita Stănescu, The Angel With A Book In His Hands*. Maşina de scris. pp. 8. ISBN 9789739929745.

[187] " Sounds Like Canada feat. Gheorghe Zamfir (http://www.cbc.ca/insite/SOUNDS_LIKE_CANADA/2006/1/17.html)". CBC Radio. 2006-01-17. . Retrieved 2008-08-31.

[188] " Gheorghe Zamfir, master of the pan pipe (http://www.gheorghe-zamfir.com/English/diskographie-e.htm)". Gheorghe Zamfir, Official Homepage. . Retrieved 2008-01-20.

[189] " Cannes 2007 Winners (http://www.altfg.com/blog/film-festivals/cannes-2007-winners/)". Alternative Film Guide. . Retrieved 2008-08-31.

[190] Jay Weissberg (2007-05-17). " 4 Months, 3 Weeks & 2 Days (http://www.variety.com/index.asp?layout=cannes2007&jump=review& reviewid=VE1117933650)". *Variety*. . Retrieved 2008-08-31.

[191] " Official list of WHS within Romania (http://whc.unesco.org/en/list/?search=&searchSites=&search_by_country=romania&type=& media=&region=&order=&criteria_restrication=&x=0&y=0)". UNESCO. . Retrieved 2008-01-31.

[192] " World Heritage List from Romania (http://www.cimec.ro/Monumente/unesco/UNESCOen/fastvers.htm)". UNESCO. . Retrieved 2008-01-31.

[193] " World Heritage Site - Romania (http://www.worldheritagesite.org/countries/romania.html)". . Retrieved 2008-01-31.

[194] Law no. 75 of 16 July 1994, published in *Monitorul Oficial* no. 237 of 26 August 1994.

[195] Governmental Decision no. 1157/2001, published in *Monitorul Oficial* no. 776 of 5 December 2001.

[196] " 'Identical flag' causes flap in Romania (http://news.bbc.co.uk/2/hi/europe/3626821.stm)". bbc.co.uk. . Retrieved 2009-09-07.

[197] "Romania". *The Europa World Year Book*. **2**. Routledge. 2007.

[198] " european-football-statistics.co.uk EFS Attendances (http://www.european-football-statistics.co.uk/attn.htm)". *European Football Statistics*. european-football-statistics.co.uk. Retrieved 2008-08-31.

[199] " Hagi leaves Romania post (http://news.bbc.co.uk/sport1/hi/football/world_cup_2002/1677201.stm)". BBC Sport. 2001-11-26. . Retrieved 2008-08-31. "Hagi enjoyed legendary status in Romania where he spearheaded the 'Golden Generation' of players..."

[200] " Hagi snubs Maradona (http://news.bbc.co.uk/sport2/low/football/europe/1264097.stm)". BBC Sport Online. 2001-04-06. . Retrieved 2008-08-31.

[201] Romanians were for example stereotyped as gymnasts, as in the South Park episode Quintuplets 2000

[202] Robin Herman (1976-03-28). " Gymnast Posts Perfect Mark (http://www.gymn-forum.net/Articles/NYT-1976_AmCup2.html)". New York Times. . Retrieved 2008-08-13.

[203] " All-Time Medal Standings, 1896-2004 (http://www.infoplease.com/ipsa/A0115108.html)". infoplease.com. . Retrieved 2008-08-31.

External links

Government

- Chief of State and Cabinet Members (https://www.cia.gov/library/publications/world-leaders-1/world-leaders-r/romania.html)
- Romanian Government (http://www.gov.ro/main/index/l/2/)
- Romanian Precidency (http://www.presidency.ro/)
- Romanian Parliament (http://www.parlament.ro/index_en.html)
- The Constitutional Court Of Romania (http://www.ccr.ro/default.aspx?lang=EN)

General information

- Country Profile (http://news.bbc.co.uk/1/hi/world/europe/country_profiles/1057466.stm) from BBC News
- Romania (https://www.cia.gov/library/publications/the-world-factbook/geos/ro.html) entry at *The World Factbook*
- Romania (http://www.state.gov/p/eur/ci/ro/) information from the United States Department of State
- Portals to the World (http://www.loc.gov/rr/international/european/romania/ro.html) from the United States Library of Congress
- Romania (http://ucblibraries.colorado.edu/govpubs/for/romania.htm) at *UCB Libraries GovPubs*
- Romania (http://www.dmoz.org/Regional/Europe/Romania/) at the Open Directory Project
- Wikimedia Atlas of Romania

Economy and law links

- Exchange Rates (http://www.bnro.ro/En/Info/curs_ext.asp) – from the National Bank of Romania
- Romanian Law and Miscellaneous - English (http://www.dreptonline.ro/resurse/resource.php)

Culture and history links

- Chronology of Romania from the World History Database (http://www.badley.info/history/Romania.index.html)
- ICI.ro - A comprehensive site about Romania (http://www.ici.ro/romania/en/index.html)
- Treasures of the national library of Romania (http://www.theeuropeanlibrary.org/portal/libraries/Libraries.php?launch=1&language=en&page=Treasures&country=Romania)

Romania around the world

- List of Romanian Meetups Worldwide (http://en.wikipedia.org/wiki/List_of_Romanian_Meetups_Worldwide)

Travel

- Romania travel guide from Wikitravel
- Official Romanian Tourism Website (http://www.romaniatourism.com/)

ace:Rumania mhr:Румыний

Communist Romania

WARNING: Article could not be rendered - ouputting plain text.

Potential causes of the problem are: (a) a bug in the pdf-writer software (b) problematic Mediawiki markup (c) table is too wide

Republica Socialistă România[1] Socialist Republic of RomaniaKingdom of Romania← 1947–1989 Romania→FlagCoat of arms Flag Coat of arms National anthemAnthemZdrobite cătuşe (1947–1953) Te slăvim Românie (1953–1977) Trei Culori (1977–1989)Location of RomaniaList of former national capitalsCapital Bucharest Language(s)Romanian languageRomanianGovernmentGovernmentSocialist republic, Single-party stateSingle-party communist stateList of Presidents of RomaniaHead of State - 1947–1952 Constantin Parhon - 1952–1958 Petru Groza - 1958–1961 Ion Gheorghe Maurer - 1961–1965 Gheorghe Gheorghiu-Dej - 1965–1967 Chivu Stoica - 1967–1989 Nicolae CeauşescuLegislatureGreat National AssemblyHistorical era Cold War - Monarchy abolished 30 December 1947 - Romanian Revolution of 1989Fall of Ceauşescu22 December 1989 List of countries and outlying territories by areaArea - 1987 238391 km² (92043 sq mi)List of countries by populationPopulation - 1987 est. 23102000 Population densityDensity 96.9 /km² (251 /sq mi) Currency Romanian Leu List of country calling codesCalling code+40[1] Until 1965 the official name was Republica Populară Romînă (People's Republic of Romania). The administrative divisions of the country were judeţe from 1947 to 1950, Administrative divisions of the Peoples' Republic of Romaniarayons from 1950 to 1968 and judeţe from 1968 to 1989.Romania, 1989Communist Romania refers to the period in Romanian history (1947-1989) when that country was a dictatorship in the Eastern Bloc led by the Romanian Communist Party, the sole legal party. Officially, the country was called the Romanian People's Republic (Romanian languageRomanian: Republica Populară Romînă; RPR) from 1947 to 1965, and the Socialist Republic of Romania (Republica Socialistă România; RSR) from 1965 to 1989.After World War II, the Soviet Union pressed for inclusion of Romania's formerly illegal Communist Party in the post-war government, while non-communist political leaders were steadily eliminated from political life. Michael of RomaniaKing Michael abdicated under pressure and went into exile in December 1947, and the Romanian People's Republic was declared. During the early years, Romania's scarce resources after World War II were drained by the "SovRom" agreements: mixed Soviet-Romanian companies established in the aftermath of World War II to mask the looting of Romania by the Soviet Union, in addition to excessive war reparations paid to the USSR. A large number of people were executed or died in custody; while judicial executions from 1945 to 1964 numbered 137,Balazs Szalontai, "The dynamic of repression: The global impact of the Stalinist model, 1944-1953", Association for Asian Research, September 9, 2003 deaths in custody are estimated in the tens of thousandsTony Judt, Postwar (book)Postwar: A History of Europe Since 1945, Penguin Press, 2005. ISBN 1-59420-065-3. "In addition to well over a million in detainees in prison, labor camps, and slave labor on the Danube-Black Sea Canal, of whom tens of thousands died and whose numbers don't include those Flight and expulsion of Germans from Romania during and after World War IIdeported to the Soviet Union, Romania was remarkable for the severity of its prison conditions". or the hundreds of thousands.Adrian Cioroianu, Pe umerii lui Marx. O introducere în istoria comunismului românesc, Editura Curtea Veche, Bucharest, 2005. ISBN 9736691756. During debates over the overall number of victims of the Communist regime between 1947 and 1964, Corneliu Coposu spoke of 282,000 arrests and 190,000 deaths in custody.Grigore Caraza, "Aiud însângerat", Bucharest: Editura Vremea XXI, 2004. ISBN 973-645-050-3. The text says: "This is how hundreds of thousands of people were killed in the terrible communist prisons"; in the prison of Aiud alone there were 625 political prisoners who were starved to death from 1945 to 1964 Anne Applebaum, Gulag: A History, Doubleday, April, 2003. ISBN 0-7679-0056-1. The author gives an estimate of 200,000 dead at the Danube-Black Sea Canal alone. Many more were imprisoned for political, economical or other reasons. There were a large number of abuses, deaths and incidents of torture against a large range of people.In the early 1960s, Romania's communist government began to assert some independence from the Soviet Union. Nicolae Ceaușescu became head of the Communist Party in 1965 and head of state in 1967, assuming the newly-established role of President of Romania in 1974. Ceaușescu's denunciation of the 1968 Soviet invasion of Czechoslovakia and a brief relaxation in internal repression helped give him a positive image both at home and in the West. Rapid economic growth fueled by foreign credits gradually gave way to austerity and political repression that led to the fall of the communist regime in December 1989. Rise of the CommunistsMain article: Soviet occupation of RomaniaSoviet occupation of Romania When Michael of RomaniaKing Michael, supported by the main political parties, overthrew Ion Antonescu in August 1944, breaking Romania away from the Axis PowersAxis and bringing it over to the AlliesAllied side, Michael could do nothing to erase the memory of his country's recent active participation in the Operation BarbarossaGerman invasion of the Soviet Union. Romanian forces fought under Soviet command, driving through Northern Transylvania into Hungary proper, and on into Czechoslovakia, Austria and Germany. However, the Soviets treated Romania as conquered territory, and Soviet troops remained in the country as occupying forces under the pretext that Romanian authorities could not guarantee the security and stability of Northern Transylvania. History of RomaniaCoat of arms of RomaniaThis article is part of a seriesPrehistory of Southeastern EuropePrehistoryDaciaDacian WarsRoman DaciaThraco-RomanRomania in the Early Middle AgesEarly Middle AgesOrigin of the RomaniansRomania in the Middle AgesMiddle AgesHistory of TransylvaniaPrincipality of TransylvaniaFoundation of WallachiaFoundation of MoldaviaEarly Modern RomaniaEarly Modern TimesPhanariotesNational awakening of RomaniaNational awakeningRegulamentul OrganicOrganic StatuteMoldavian Revolution of 18481848 Moldavian RevolutionWallachian Revolution of 18481848 Wallachian RevolutionUnited PrincipalitiesRomanian War of IndependenceWar of IndependenceKingdom of RomaniaRomania during World War IWorld War IGreater RomaniaRomania during World War IIWorld War IISoviet occupation of Bessarabia and Northern BukovinaCommunist RomaniaSoviet occupation of RomaniaSoviet occupationRomanian Revolution of 19891989 RevolutionHistory of Romania since 1989Romania since 1989TopicTimeline of Romanian historyTimelineMilitary history of RomaniaMilitary historyRomania PortalThe Yalta Conference had granted the Soviet Union a predominant interest in Romania, the Paris Peace Treaties failed to acknowledge Romania as a co-belligerenceco-belligerent, and the Red Army was sitting on Romanian soil. The Communists played only a minor role in Michael's wartime government, headed by General Nicolae Rădescu, but this changed in March 1945, when Dr. Petru Groza of the Ploughmen's Front, a party closely associated with the Communists, became prime minister. Although his government was broad, including members of most major prewar parties except the Iron Guard, the Communists held the key ministries. The King was not happy with the direction of this government, but when he attempted to force Groza's resignation by refusing to sign any legislation (a move known as "the royal strike"), Groza simply chose to enact laws without bothering to obtain Michael's signature. On November 8, 1945, King Michael's name day, an anti-communismanti-communist demonstration in front of the National Museum of Art of RomaniaRoyal Palace in Bucharest was met with force, resulting in dozens of killed and wounded; Soviet officers restrained Romanian soldiers and police from firing on civilians, and Soviet troops restored order.David R. Stone, "The 1945 Ethridge Mission to Bulgaria and Romania and the Origins of the Cold War in the Balkans", Diplomacy & Statecraft, Volume 17, no. 1, March 2006, pp. 93–112.Despite the King's disapproval, the first Groza government brought Land reform in Romanialand reform and women's suffrage. However, it also brought the beginnings of Soviet domination of Romania. In the Romanian general election, 1946elections of November 19, 1946, Communists claimed by electoral fraud 80% of the votes given under Soviet military pressure and diversions. After forming government, the Communists worked to eliminate the role of the centrist parties; notably, the National Peasant Party was accused of espionage after it became clear in 1947 that their leaders were meeting secretly with United States officials. A show trial of their leadership was then arranged, and they were put in jail. Other parties were forced to "merge" with the Communists. In 1946-7, hundreds of participants in the pro-Axis regime were executed as war criminals, primarily for their involvement in the Holocaust and for attacking the Soviet Union. Antonescu himself was executed June 1, 1946. By 1948, most non-Communist politicians were either executed, in exile or in prison. Romania remained the only monarchy in the Eastern Bloc by 1947. On December 30 of that year, the Communists forced King Michael to abdicationabdicate. The Communists declared a People's Republic, formalized with the constitution of April 13, 1948. The new constitution forbade and punished any association which had "fascist or anti-democratic nature". It also granted the freedom of press, speech and assembly for the working class. In the face of wide-scale killings, imprisonments and harassment of local peasants during forced collectivization, entire private property nationalization and political oppressiveness, the Constitution of 1948 and the subsequent basic texts were never respected by governments or the new judges appointed during dictatorship. The Communist government also disbanded the Romanian Greek-Catholic Uniate Church, declaring its merger with the Romanian Orthodox Church. Early years of the communist state See also: Romanian anti-communist resistance movementResistance in the early years The early years of Communist rule in Romania were marked by repeated changes of course and by numerous arrests and imprisonments as factions contended for dominance. The country's resources were also drained by the Soviet's SovRom agreements, which facilitated shipping of Romanian goods to the Soviet Union at nominal prices. In all ministries there were Soviet "advisers" who reported directly to Moscow and held the real decision-making powers. All walks of life were infiltrated by agents and informers of the secret police. In 1948 the earlier agrarian reform was reversed, replaced by a move toward collective farming. This resulted in forced Collectivization in Romaniacollectivization, since wealthier peasants generally did not want to give up their land voluntarily, and had to be "convinced" by beatings, intimidation, arrests and deportations. On June 11, 1948, all banks and large businesses were nationalized. In the Communist leadership, there appear to have been three important factions, all of them Stalinist, differentiated more by their respective personal histories than by any deep political or philosophical differences: The "Muscovites", notably Ana Pauker and Vasile Luca, had spent the war in Moscow. The "Prison Communists", notably Gheorghe Gheorghiu-Dej, had been imprisoned during the war. The somewhat less firmly Stalinist "Secretariat Communists", notably Lucreţiu Pătrăşcanu had made it through the Antonescu years by hiding within Romania and had participated in the broad governments immediately after Romania during World War II#the royal coupKing Michael's 1944 coup. Ultimately, with Joseph Stalin's backing, and probably due in part to the anti-Semitic policies of late Stalinism (Pauker was Jewish), Gheorghiu-Dej and the "Prison Communists" won out. Pauker was purged from the party (along with 192,000 other party members); Pătrăşcanu was executed after a show trial. The Gheorghiu-Dej era Gheorghe Gheorghiu-DejGheorghiu-Dej, a firm Stalinist, was not pleased with the reforms in Nikita Khrushchev's Soviet Union after Stalin's death in 1953. He also blanched at Comecon's goal of turning Romania into the "breadbasket" of the East Bloc, pursuing a program of the development of heavy industry. He also closed Romania's largest labor camps, abandoned the Danube–Black Sea Canal project, halted rationing and hiked workers' wages. Further, there was continuing resentment that historically Romanian lands remained part of the Soviet Union as the Moldavian SSR. These factors combined to put Romania under Gheorghiu-Dej on a relatively independent and nationalist route. Gheorghiu-Dej identified with Stalinism, and the more liberal Soviet regime threatened to undermine his authority. In an effort to reinforce his position, Gheorghiu-Dej pledged cooperation with any state, regardless of political-economic system, as long as it recognized international equality and did not interfere in other nations' domestic affairs. This policy led to a tightening of Romania's bonds with China, which also advocated national self-determination. Gheorghiu-Dej resigned as the party's general secretary in 1954 but retained the premiership; a four-member collective secretariat, including Nicolae Ceauşescu, controlled the party for a year before Gheorghiu-Dej again took up the reins. Despite its new policy of international cooperation, Romania joined the Warsaw Treaty Organization (Warsaw Pact) in 1955, which entailed subordinating and integrating a portion of its military into the Soviet military machine. Romania later refused to allow Warsaw Pact maneuvers on its soil and limited its participation in military maneuvers elsewhere within the alliance. In 1956, the Soviet premier, Nikita Khrushchev, denounced Stalin in a Secret Speechsecret speech before the Twentieth Congress of the Communist Party of the Soviet Union (CPSU). Gheorghiu-Dej and the leadership of the Romanian Workers' Party (Partidul Muncitoresc Român, PMR) were fully braced to weather de-Stalinization. Gheorghiu-Dej made

Pauker, Luca and Georgescu scapegoats for the Romanian communists' past excesses and claimed that the Romanian party had purged its Stalinist elements even before Stalin had died.In October 1956, Poland's communist leaders refused to succumb to Soviet military threats to intervene in domestic political affairs and install a more obedient politburo. A few weeks later, the Communist Party in Hungary virtually disintegrated during a popular revolution. Poland's Polish Octoberdefiance and Hungary's popular uprising inspired Romanian students and workers to demonstrate in university and industrial towns calling for liberty, better living conditions, and an end to Soviet domination. Under the pretext that the Hungarian uprising might incite his nation's own revolt, Gheorghiu-Dej took radical measures which meant persecutions and jailing of various "suspects", especially people of Hungarian origin. He also advocated swift Soviet intervention, and the Soviet Union reinforced its military presence in Romania, particularly along the Hungarian border. Although Romania's unrest proved fragmentary and controllable, Hungary's was not, so in November Moscow mounted a Hungarian Revolution of 1956bloody invasion of Hungary. Romania and Yugoslavia both offered to take part in the military intervention in Hungary in 1956, but Nikita Khruschev rejected them. After the Revolution of 1956, Gheorghiu-Dej worked closely with Hungary's new leader, Janos Kadar, who was installed by the Soviet Union. Romania took Hungary's former premier (leader of the 1956 revolution) Imre Nagy into custody. He was jailed at Snagov, north of Bucharest. After a series of interrogations by Soviets and Romanian authorities, Nagy was returned to Budapest for trial and execution. In Transylvania, the Romanian authorities merged Hungarian languageHungarian and Romanian languageRomanian universities at Cluj-NapocaCluj, putting an end to the Hungarian Bolyai University, and also worked on gradually eliminating Hungarian education in middle schools by transforming them into Romanian ones. Under the pretext of calling numerous ethnic Hungarians "irredentists" who were "dangers to Romania's territorial integrity", the communist regime led by Gheorghiu-Dej jailed a large number of Hungarians, as well as executing some. During his 2007 visit, Hungarian president Laszlo Solyom asked for the rehabilitation of the politically persecuted Hungarians, among whom were numerous poets, writers, university teachers. The Hungarian president also mentioned that 20 Hungarians were executed and that over 40 thousand years of jail were given in total to ethnic Hungarians. The request for rehabilitation of the politically persecuted Hungarians was not taken into consideration by the Romanian side.Gheorghiu-Dej spread fears about Hungary wanting to take over Transylvania. He took a two-pronged approach to the problem, arresting the leaders of the Hungarian People's Alliance, but, under Soviet pressure, establishing a nominally Hungarian Autonomous Provinceautonomous Hungarian region in the Szekely land. Romania's government also took measures to allay domestic discontent by reducing investments in heavy industry, boosting output of consumer goods, decentralizing economic management, hiking wages and incentives, and instituting elements of worker management. The authorities eliminated compulsory deliveries for private farmers but reaccelerated the collectivization program in the mid-1950s, albeit less brutally than earlier. The government declared collectivization complete in 1962, when collective and state farms controlled 77% of the arable land. Despite Gheorghiu-Dej's claim that he had purged the Romanian party of Stalinists, he remained susceptible to attack for his obvious complicity in the party's activities from 1944 to 1953. At a plenary PMR meeting in March 1956, Miron Constantinescu and Iosif Chişinevschi, both Politburo members and deputy premiers, criticized Gheorghiu-Dej. Constantinescu, who advocated a Khrushchev-style liberalization, posed a particular threat to Gheorghiu-Dej because he enjoyed good connections with the Moscow leadership. The PMR purged Constantinescu and Chişinevschi in 1957, denouncing both as Stalinists and charging them with complicity with Pauker. Afterwards, Gheorghiu-Dej faced no serious challenge to his leadership. Ceauşescu replaced Constantinescu as head of PMR cadres. Some Romanian Jews initially favored Communism, in reaction to the anti-Semitism of the Fascists during World War II. However, by the 1950s, most were disappointed with the increasing discrimination of the Party and the limitations for Aliyahemigration to Israel. Persecution, the labor camp system and anti-communist resistance Main articles: Romanian anti-communist resistance movementRomanian anti-communist resistance movement, Bărăgan deportationsBărăgan deportations, and Piteşti prisonPiteşti prison Harsh persecutions of any real or imagined enemies of the Communist regime started with the Soviet occupation in 1945. The Soviet army behaved as an occupation force (although theoretically it was an ally against Nazi Germany), and could arrest virtually anyone at will, for perceived "fascist" or "anti-Soviet" activities. The occupation period was marked by frequent rapes, looting and brutality against the civilian population.Shortly after Soviet occupation, ethnic Germans (who were Romanian citizens and had been living as a community in Romania for 800 years) were deported to the Donbas coal mines (see Flight and expulsion of Germans from Romania during and after World War II). Despite the King's protest, who pointed out that this was against international law, an estimated 70,000 men and women were forced to leave their homes, starting in January 1945, before the war had even ended. They were loaded in cattle cars and put to work in the Soviet mines for up to ten years as "reparations", where about one in five died from disease, accidents and malnutrition. Once the Communist regime became more entrenched, the number of arrests increased. All strata of society were involved, but particularly targeted were the pre-war elites, such as intellectuals, clerics, teachers, former politicians (even if they had left-leaning views) and anybody who could potentially form the nucleus of anti-Communist resistance. The existing prisons were filled with political prisoners, and a new system of forced labor camps and prisons was created, modeled after the Soviet Gulag. A futile project to dig the Danube-Black Sea Canal served as a pretext for the erection of several labor camps, where numerous people died. Some of the most notorious prisons included Sighet, Gherla, Piteşti and Aiud, and forced labor camps were set up at lead mines and in the Danube Delta. The Piteşti prisonprison in Piteşti was the epicenter of a particularly vicious communist "experiment" during this era. It involved both psychological and physical torture, resulting in the total breakdown of the individual. The ultimate aim was to force prisoners to "confess" to imaginary crimes or "denounce" themselves and others, therefore prolonging their prison sentences. This "experiment" resulted in numerous suicides inside the prison and was ultimately stopped. The Stalinist measures of the Communist government included Bărăgan deportationsdeportation of peasants from the Banat (south-east Transylvania, at the border with Yugoslavia), started on June 18, 1951. About 45,000 people were given two hours to collect their belongings, loaded up in cattle cars under armed guard, and were then forcibly "resettled" in barren spots on the eastern plains (Bărăgan PlainBărăgan). This was meant as an intimidation tactic to force the remaining peasants to join collective farms. Most deportees lived in the Bărăgan for 5 years (until 1956), but some remained there permanently. Anti-communist resistance also had an organized form, and many people opposing the regime took up arms and formed partisan groups, comprising 10-40 people. There were attacks on police posts and sabotage. Some of the famous partisans were Elisabeta Rizea from Nucşoara and Gheorghe Arsenescu. Despite a large number of secret police (Securitate) and army troops massed against them, armed resistance in the mountains continued until the early 1960s, and one of the best known partisan leaders was not captured until 1974.Another form of anti-communist resistance, non-violent this time, was the Bucharest student movement of 1956student movement of 1956. In reaction to the anti-communist revolt in Hungary, echoes were felt all over the Eastern bloc. Protests took place in some university centers resulting in numerous arrests and expulsions. The most organized student movement was in Timişoara, where 3000 were arrested." Trei mii de studenţi timişoreni, arestaţi şi torturaţi", România liberă, 25 October 2007. In Bucharest and Cluj, organized groups were set up which tried to make common cause with the anti-communist movement in Hungary and coordinate activity. The authorities' reaction was immediate - students were arrested or suspended from their courses, some teachers were dismissed, and new associations were set up to supervise student activities. The Ceauşescu regime The Coat of Arms of The Socialist Republic of Romania (1965–89)Gheorghiu-Dej died in 1965 in unclear circumstances (his death apparently occurred when he was in Moscow for medical treatment) and, after the inevitable power struggle, was succeeded by the previously obscure Nicolae Ceauşescu. Where Gheorghiu-Dej had hewed to a Stalinist line while the Soviet Union was in a reformist period, Ceauşescu initially appeared to be a reformist, precisely as the Soviet Union was headed into its Neo-Stalinismneo-Stalinist era under Leonid Brezhnev. Gheorghiu-Dej exploited the Russian - Chinese dispute in his last two years and began to oppose the hegemony of the Soviet Union from a Romanian national position. Ceauşescu, supported by a part of the former collaborators of Gheorghiu-Dej, like Maurer, continued this line which was naturally very popular in the country. The relations with Western countries, but also with many other states, began to be strengthened in what seemed to be the national interest of Romania. The forced Soviet (mostly Russian) cultural influence in the country which characterized the fifties was stopped. The first yearsIn 1965, following the example of Czechoslovakia, the name of the country was changed to Republica Socialistă România (The Socialist Republic of Romania) — RSR — and PMR was renamed once again to Partidul Communist Român — The Romanian Communist Party (PCR). In his early years in power, Ceaușescu was genuinely popular, both at home and abroad. Agricultural goods were abundant, consumer goods began to reappear, there was a cultural thaw, and, most importantly abroad, he spoke out against the 1968 Soviet invasion of Czechoslovakia. While his reputation at home soon paled, he continued to have uncommonly good relations with Western governments and with institutions such as the International Monetary Fund and World Bank because of his independent political line. Romania under Ceaușescu maintained and sometimes improved diplomatic and other relations with, among others, West Germany, Israel, China, Albania, Pinochet's Chile, all for various reasons on the outs with Moscow. Human rights issuesHowever, even at the start, reproductive freedom was severely restricted. Wishing to increase the birth rate, in 1966, Ceaușescu promulgated the decree 770 abortion in Romaniarestricting abortion and contraception: only women over the age of 45 who had at least four children were eligible   for   either;   in   1989,   the   number   was   increased   to   five children.http://www.nytimes.com/1990/06/24/magazine/romania-s-lost-children-a-photo-essay-by-james-nachtwey.html Mandatory gynecological revisions and penalizations against unmarried women and childless couples completed the natalist measures. The birthrate of 1967 was almost double the one of 1966, leaving a decrețeidecreței cohort who suffered because of crowded public services.Other restrictions of human rights were typical of a Stalinist regime: a massive force of secret police (the "Securitate"), censorship, relocation, but not on the same scale as in the 1950s. Heavy industrialisationDuring the Ceaușescu era, there was a secret ongoing "trade" between Romania on one side and Israel and West Germany on the other side, under which Israel and West Germany paid money to Romania to allow Romanian citizens with certified Jewish or German ancestry to emigrate to Israel and West Germany, respectively. 23 August parade Ceaușescu's Romania continued to pursue Gheorghiu-Dej's policy of industrialization, but still produced few goods of a quality suitable for the world market. Also, after a visit to North Korea, Ceaușescu developed a megalomaniacal vision of completely remaking the country; this became known as systematization (Romania)systematization. A significant portion of the capital, Bucharest, was torn down to make way for the Palace of the ParliamentCasa Poporului (now House of Parliament) complex and Centrul Civic (Civic Center), but the Romanian Revolution of 1989December 1989 Revolution left much of the huge complex unfinished, such as a new National Library and the National Museum of History. During the huge demolitions in the 1980s, this area was popularly called "Ceaușima" - a bitter satirical allusion of Ceaușescu and HiroshimaLonely Planet, Romania - Dracula romanticism and a country on fast-forward, accessed on October 18, 2006. Currently it is being redeveloped as a commercial area known as Esplanada. Prior to the mid-1970s, Bucharest, as most other cities, was developed by expanding the city, especially towards the south, east and west, by building high density dormitory neighborhoods at the outskirts of the city, some (such as Drumul Taberei, Berceni, Titan or Giurgiului) of architectural and urban planning value. Conservation plans were made, especially during the 1960s and early 1970s, but all was halted, after Ceaușescu embarked on what is known as "The Small Cultural Revolution" ("Mica revoluție culturală"), after visiting North Korea and the People's Republic of China and then delivering a speech known as the July Theses. In the late 1970s, the construction of the Bucharest Metro system was started. After two years, 10 km of network were already completely and after another 2 years, 9 km of tunnels were ready for use. By 17th of August 1989, 49.01 km of the subway system and 34 stations were already in use. The 1977 Bucharest Earthquakebig earthquake of 1977 shocked Bucharest, many buildings collapsed, and many others were weakened. This was the backdrop that led to a policy of large-scale demolition which affected monuments of historical significance or architectural masterpieces such as the monumental Văcărești Monastery (1722), the "Sfânta Vineri" (1645) and "Enei" (1611) Churches, the Cotroceni (1679) and Pantelimon (1750) Monasteries, the art deco "Republic's Stadium" (ANEF Stadium, 1926). Even the Palace of Justice — built by Romania's foremost architect, Ion Mincu, was scheduled for demolition in early 1990, according to the systematisation papers. Yet another tactic was abandoning and neglecting buildings and bringing them into such a state that they would require being torn down. Thus, the policy towards the city after the earthquake was not one of reconstruction, but one of demolition and building anew. Post-earthquake estimates commissioned by the office of the city's mayor judged that only 23 buildings were beyond repair, none of them of any historic value. An analysis by the Union of Architects, commissioned in 1990, claims that over 2000 buildings were torn down, with over 77 of very high architectural importance, most of them in good condition. Even Gara de Nord (the city's main train station), listed on the Romanian Architectural Heritage List, was scheduled to be torn down and replaced in early 1992. Despite all of this, and despite the appalling treatment of HIV-infected orphans, the country continued to have a notably good system of schools. Also, not every industrialization project was a failure: Ceauşescu left Romania with a reasonably effective system of power generation and transmission, gave Bucharest Bucharest Metroa functioning subway, and left many cities with an increase in habitable apartment buildings. A queue for cooking oil, Bucharest, late 1980sThe 1980s: severe rationing and construction of the Palace of the PeopleIn the 1980s, Ceauşescu became simultaneously obsessed with repaying Western loans and with building himself a Palace of the People (Romania)palace of unprecedented proportions, along with an equally grandiose neighborhood, Centrul Civic, to accompany it. These led to a shortage of available goods for the average Romanian. By 1984, despite high crop yield and food production, food rationing was introduced on a wide scale (the government promoted it as "a means to reduce obesity" and "rational eating"). Bread, milk, butter, cooking oil, sugar, pork, beef, chicken, and in some places even potatoes were rationed in most of Romania by 1989, with rations being made smaller every year (by 1989, a person could legally buy only 10 eggs per month, half to one loaf of bread per day, depending on the place of residence, or 500 grams of any kind of meat). Most of what was available were export rejects, as most of the quality goods were exported, even underpriced, in order to obtain hard currency, either to pay the debt, or to push forward in the ever-growing pursuits of heavy industrialisation. Romanians became accustomed to "tacâmuri de pui" (chicken wings, claws and so on), mixed cooking oil (mostly unrefined, dark, soy oil, of the poorest grade), "Bucureşti Salami" (consisting of soy, bonemeal, offal and pork lard), ersatz coffee (made of corn), oceanic fish and sardines as a meat replacement, cheese mixed with starch or flour, untasty juices as Cil-Cola or Cireşica . Even these products were in very scarce supply, with queues whenever such products were available. All quality products, such as Sibiu SalamiSibiu and Victoria Salami, high- and mid-grade meats, and Dobrudja peaches were designated as "export-only", and were available to Romanians only on the thriving black market.By 1985, despite Romania's huge refining capacity, petrol was strictly rationed, with supplies drastically cut, a Sunday curfew was instated, and many buses and taxis converted to methane propulsion (they were mockingly named "bombs"). Electricity was rationed to divert supplies to heavy industry, with a maximum monthly allowed consumption of 20 Kilowatt hourkWh per family (everything over this limit was heavily taxed), and very frequent Rolling blackoutblackouts (generally 1–2 hours daily). Only one in five streetlights were to be kept on, and television was reduced to a 2 hours each day, mostly propaganda. A propaganda poster on the streets of Bucharest, 1986. The caption reads "65 years since the creation of the Romanian Communist Party", while in the background it reads "Ceauşescu Era" and "The Party. Ceauşescu. Romania" Gas and heating were also turned off; people in cities had to turn to natural gas containers ("butelii"), or charcoal stoves, even though they were connected to the gas mains. According to a decree of 1988, all public spaces had to be kept to a temperature of no more than 16 degrees Celsius (about 63 degrees Fahrenheit) in winter (the only institutions exempted were kindergartens and hospitals), with some (such as factories), kept at no more than 14 degrees (about 59 degrees Fahrenheit). All shops were to close no later than 5:30 p.m., in order to preserve electricity. A thriving black market appeared, with Kent (cigarette)Kent cigarettes becoming Romania's second currency (it was illegal and punished with up to ten years imprisonment to own or trade any foreign currency), used to purchase everything, from food to clothes or medicine. Health care dropped substantially, as drugs were no longer imported.The last years: increased control over societyControl over society became stricter and stricter, with an East GermanyEast German-style Telephone tapping in the Eastern Blocphone bugging system installed, and with Securitate recruiting more agents, extending censorship and keeping tabs and records on a large segment of the population. By 1989, according to CNSAS (the Council for Studies of the Archives of the Former Securitate), one in three Romanians was an informant for the Securitate. Due to this state of affairs, income from tourism dropped substantially, the number of foreign tourists visiting Romania dropping by 75%, with the three main tour operators that organized trips in Romania leaving the country by 1987. There was also a revival of the effort to build: a Danube–Black Sea Canal, which was completed, a nationwide canal system and irrigation network, some of which was completed, but most of which still a project, or abandoned, an effort to improve the railway system with electrification and a modern control system, a nuclear reactornuclear power plant at Cernavodă, a national hydroelectricityhydroelectric power system, including the Iron Gate (Danube)Porţile de Fier power station on the Danube in cooperation with Socialist Federal Republic of YugoslaviaYugoslavia, a network of oil refineries, a fairly developed oceanic fishing fleet, naval shipyards at Constanţa, a good industrial basis for the chemical and heavy machinery industries, and a rather well-developed foreign policy. The regime's legacy On the negative side, the legacy of the period was a bloated heavy industry using archaic production methods, consuming lots of resources, and producing low-value goods (the refining capacity is over ten times what was needed, the steel production capabilities two-and-a-half times, the aluminium production facilities five times). Most of what was produced could not be sold anywhere, and ended up sitting and deteriorating outside the factories where it was made, while light industries were ridiculously undersized (Romanians had to wait three years for a washing machine, two-to-three years for a color TV, five-to-ten years for a car), and technologically obsolete (in 1989, Romania, produced 1960s cars and 1970s TVs and washing machines). The communication network was, with the exception of the modernization of the trunk railway lines, left at the 1950s level. The telephone network was one of the least reliable in Europe, with 1930s–1950s manual telephone switchsswitching technologies in villages, and early 1960s automatic switching in towns and cities, and based on an under-sized backbone. By 1989, in Romania, there were about 700,000 phone lines, for a population of 23 million. TV broadcasts were limited to two hours daily, mostly propaganda, with most people choosing to watch Bulgarian televisionBulgarian, Yugoslavian Radio TelevisionYugoslavian, Hungarian televisionHungarian or Soviet televisionSoviet Russian TV, wherever the signal was sufficiently strong, using illegal antennas or mini satellite dishes. There were almost no computers, 8-bit clones of Western home computers being directly shipped to serve as workstations in factories and such.Another legacy of this era was pollution: Ceauşescu's government scored badly on this count even by the standards of the Eastern European communist states. Examples include Copşa Mică with its infamous Carbon Powder factory (in the 1980s, the whole city could be seen from satellite as covered by a thick black cloud), Hunedoara, or the plan, launched in 1989, to convert the unique Danube Delta — a UNESCO World Heritage site — to plain agricultural fields. Downfall Main articles: Braşov RebellionBraşov Rebellion and Romanian Revolution of 1989Romanian Revolution of 1989 Unlike the Soviet Union at the same time, Romania did not develop a large, privileged elite. Outside of Ceauşescu's own relatives, government officials were frequently rotated from one job to another and moved around geographically, to reduce the chance of anyone developing a power base. This prevented the rise of the Mikhail GorbachevGorbachev-era reformist communism found in Hungary or the Soviet Union. Similarly, unlike in Poland, Ceauşescu reacted to strikes entirely through a strategy of further oppression. Romania was nearly the last of the Eastern European communist regimes to fall; its fall was also the most violent up to that time. The events of December 1989 are much in dispute. Protests and riots broke out in Timişoara on December 17 and soldiers opened fire on the protesters, killing about 100 people. After cutting short a two-day trip to Iran, Ceauşescu held a televised speech on December 20, in which he condemned the events of Timişoara, considering them an act of foreign intervention in the internal affairs of Romania and an aggression through foreign secret services on Romania's sovereignty, and declared National Curfew, convoking a mass meeting in his support in Bucharest for the next day. The uprising of Timişoara became known across the country, and in the morning of December 21, protests spread to Sibiu, Bucharest, and elsewhere. On December 21 the meeting at the CC Building in Bucharest turned into chaos and finally into riot, Ceauşescu hiding himself in the CC Building after losing control of his own "supporters". On the morning of the next day, December 22, it was announced that the army general Vasile Milea was dead by suicide; people were besieging the CC Building, while the Securitate did nothing to help Ceauşescu. Ceauşescu soon fled in an helicopter from the rooftop of the CC Building, only to find himself abandoned in Târgovişte, where he was finally formally tried and shot by a kangaroo court on December 25. Controversy over the events of December 1989 For several months after the events of December 1989, it was widely argued that Ion Iliescu and the National Salvation Front (Romania)National Salvation Front (FSN) had merely taken advantage of the chaos to stage a coup. While, ultimately, a great deal did change in Romania, it is still very contentious among Romanians and other observers as to whether this was their intent from the outset, or merely pragmatic playing of the cards they were dealt. It is clear that by December 1989 Ceauşescu's harsh and counterproductive economic and political policies had cost him the support of many government officials and even the most loyal Communist Party cadres, most of whom joined forces with the popular revolution or simply refused to support him. This loss of support from regime officials ultimately set the stage for Ceauşescu's demise. See alsoReconstruction (2001 film)- a documentary about Communist RomaniaList of Romanian communistsScânteia - The Romanian Communist Party's newspaper The Presidential Commission for the Study of the Communist Dictatorship in RomaniaAdministrative divisions of the Peoples' Republic of RomaniaSystematization (Romania) < Romania during World War IIWorld War II I History of Romania I History of Romania since 1989Present Romania > External links Ceausescu.org, extensive website on Communist Romania. MemorialSighet.ro, memorial site to the victims of Communism in Romania, based at Sighet prison.

Nicolae Ceauşescu

<table>
<tr><td colspan="2" align="center">Nicolae Ceauşescu</td></tr>
<tr><td colspan="2" align="center"></td></tr>
<tr><td colspan="2" align="center">General Secretary of the Romanian Communist Party</td></tr>
<tr><td colspan="2" align="center">In office
22 March 1965 – 22 December 1989</td></tr>
<tr><td>Preceded by</td><td>Gheorghe Gheorghiu-Dej</td></tr>
<tr><td>Succeeded by</td><td>party abolished</td></tr>
<tr><td colspan="2" align="center">President of the State Council</td></tr>
<tr><td colspan="2" align="center">In office
9 December 1967 – 22 December 1989</td></tr>
<tr><td>Preceded by</td><td>Chivu Stoica</td></tr>
<tr><td>Succeeded by</td><td>none</td></tr>
<tr><td colspan="2" align="center">1st President of Romania</td></tr>
<tr><td colspan="2" align="center">In office
28 March 1974 – 22 December 1989</td></tr>
<tr><td>Preceded by</td><td>none</td></tr>
<tr><td>Succeeded by</td><td>Ion Iliescu</td></tr>
<tr><td>Born</td><td>26 January 1918
Scorniceşti, Olt, → Romania</td></tr>
<tr><td>Died</td><td>25 December 1989 (aged 71)
Târgovişte, Dâmboviţa, → Romania</td></tr>
<tr><td>Nationality</td><td>Romanian</td></tr>
<tr><td>Political party</td><td>Communist Party of Romania</td></tr>
<tr><td>Spouse(s)</td><td>Elena Ceauşescu</td></tr>
<tr><td>Children</td><td>Valentin Ceauşescu, Zoia Ceauşescu, Nicu Ceauşescu</td></tr>
<tr><td>Religion</td><td>None (AtheistWikipedia:Disputed statement)</td></tr>
<tr><td>Signature</td><td></td></tr>
</table>

Nicolae Andruţă Ceauşescu (Romanian pronunciation: [nikoˈla.e andru.t̄sa tʃa.uˈʃesku]) (26 January 1918 – 25 December 1989) was the Secretary General of the Romanian Workers' Party, later the Romanian Communist Party from 1965 until 1989, President of the Council of State from 1967 and President of Romania from 1974 until 1989. His rule was marked in the first decade by an open policy towards Western Europe and the United States of America, which deviated from that of the other Warsaw Pact states during the Cold War. He continued a trend first established by his predecessor, Gheorghe Gheorghiu-Dej, who had tactfully coaxed the Khrushchev regime to withdraw troops from Romania in 1958.[1] Ceauşescu's second decade was characterized by an increasingly erratic personality cult, extreme nationalism and a deterioration in foreign relations with Western powers and also with the Soviet Union. Ceauşescu's government was overthrown in a military coup December 1989, and he was shot following a televised two-hour session by a kangaroo court.[2]

Early life and career

Born in the village of Scorniceşti, Olt County, Ceauşescu moved to Bucharest at the age of 11 to work in the factories. He was the son of a peasant (see Ceauşescu family for descriptions of his parents and siblings.) He joined the then-illegal Communist Party of Romania in early 1932 and was first arrested, in 1933, for agitating during a strike. He was arrested again, in 1934, first for collecting signatures on a petition protesting the trial of railway workers and twice more for other similar activities. These arrests earned him the description "dangerous communist agitator" and "active distributor of communist and anti-fascist propaganda" on his police record. He then went underground, but was captured and imprisoned in 1936 for two years at Doftana Prison for anti-fascist activities.[3]

Arrested in 1933, when he was 15 years old, for "active distribution of communist and anti-fascist propaganda"

While out of jail in 1939, he met Elena Petrescu (they married in 1946) —she would play an increasing role in his political life over the decades. He was arrested and imprisoned again in 1940. In 1943, he was transferred to Târgu Jiu internment camp where he shared a cell with Gheorghe Gheorghiu-Dej, becoming his protege. After World War II, when Romania was beginning to fall under Soviet influence, he served as secretary of the Union of Communist Youth (1944–1945).[3]

After the Communists seized power in Romania in 1947, he headed the Ministry of Agriculture, then served as Deputy Minister of the Armed Forces under Gheorghe Gheorghiu-Dej. In 1952, Gheorghiu-Dej brought him onto the Central Committee months after the party's "Muscovite faction" led by Ana Pauker had been purged. In 1954, he became a full member of the Politburo and eventually rose to occupy the second-highest position in the party hierarchy.[3]

Leadership of Romania

Three days after the death of Gheorghiu-Dej in March 1965, Ceauşescu became first secretary of the Romanian Workers' Party. One of his first acts was to change the name of the party to The Romanian Communist Party, and declare the country the → Socialist Republic of Romania rather than a People's Republic. In 1967, he consolidated his power by becoming president of the State Council.

Initially, Ceauşescu became a popular figure in Romania and also in the Western World, due to his independent foreign policy, challenging the authority of the Soviet Union. In the 1960s, he ended Romania's active participation in the Warsaw Pact (though Romania formally remained a member); he refused to take part in the 1968 invasion of Czechoslovakia by Warsaw Pact forces, and actively and openly condemned that action. Although the Soviet Union largely tolerated Ceauşescu's recalcitrance, his seeming independence from Moscow earned Romania maverick status within the Eastern Bloc.

In 1974, Ceauşescu became "President of Romania", further consolidating his power. He followed an independent policy in foreign relations—for example, in 1984, Romania was one of only three Communist-ruled countries (the others being the People's Republic of China, and Yugoslavia) to take part in the American-organized 1984 Summer Olympics. Also, the country was the first of the Eastern Bloc to have official relations with the European Community: an agreement including Romania in the Community's Generalised System of Preferences was signed in 1974 and an Agreement on Industrial Products was signed in 1980. However, Ceauşescu refused to implement any liberal reforms. The evolution of his regime followed the Stalinist path already traced by Gheorghiu-Dej. Their opposition to Soviet control was mainly determined by the unwillingness to proceed to de-Stalinization. The secret police (Securitate) maintained firm control over speech and the media, and tolerated no internal opposition.

Josip Broz Tito and Nicolae Ceauşescu

Beginning in 1972, Ceauşescu instituted a program of systematisation. Promoted as a way to build a "multilaterally developed socialist society", the program of demolition, resettlement, and construction began in the countryside, but culminated with an attempt to reshape the country's capital completely. Over one fifth of central Bucharest, including churches and historic buildings, was demolished in the 1980s, in order to rebuild the city in his own style. The People's House ("Casa Poporului") in Bucharest, now the Palace of the Parliament, is the world's second largest administrative building, after The Pentagon. Ceauşescu also planned to bulldoze many villages in order to move the peasants into blocks of flats in the cities, as part of his "urbanisation" and "industrialisation" programs. An NGO project called "Sister Villages" that created bonds between European and Romanian communities may have played a role in thwarting these plans.

Ceauşescu is greeted by King Juan Carlos I of Spain in Madrid, 1979

The 1966 decree

In 1966, the Ceauşescu regime banned all abortion, and introduced other policies to increase the very low birth rate and fertility rate - including a special tax amounting to between ten and twenty percent on the incomes of men and women who remained childless after the age of twenty-five, whether married or single. The inability to procreate due to medical reasons did not make a difference. Abortion was permitted only in cases where the woman in question was over forty-two, or already the mother of four (later five) children. Mothers of at least five children would be entitled to significant benefits, while mothers of at least ten children were declared *heroine mothers* by the → Romanian State. However, few women ever sought this status; instead, the average Romanian family during the Communist era had two to three children (see Demographics of Romania).[4] Furthermore, a considerable number of women either died or were maimed during clandestine abortions.[5]

The government also targeted rising divorce rates and made divorce much more difficult - it was decreed that a marriage could be dissolved only in exceptional cases. By the late 1960s, the population began to swell, accompanied by rising poverty and increased homelessness (street children) in the urban areas. In turn, a new problem was created by uncontrollable child abandonment, which swelled the orphanage population (See Cighid) and facilitated a rampant AIDS epidemic in the late 1980s - created by the regime's refusal to acknowledge the existence of the disease, and its unwillingness to allow for any HIV test to be carried out.[6]

July Theses

Main article: July Theses

Ceauşescu visited the People's Republic of China, North Korea and North Vietnam in 1971 and was inspired by the hardline model he found there. He took great interest in the idea of total national transformation as embodied in the programs of the Korean Workers' Party and China's Cultural Revolution. Shortly after returning home, he began to emulate North Korea's system, influenced by the Juche philosophy of North Korean President Kim Il Sung. North Korean books on Juche were translated into Romanian and widely distributed in the country. On 6 July 1971, he delivered a speech before the Executive Committee of the PCR. This quasi-Maoist speech, which came to be known as the July Theses, contained seventeen proposals. Among these were: continuous growth in the "leading role" of the

Kim Il-sung with Nicolae Ceauşescu in North Korea in 1971

Party; improvement of Party education and of mass political action; youth participation on large construction projects as part of their "patriotic work"; an intensification of political-ideological education in schools and universities, as well as in children's, youth and student organisations; and an expansion of political propaganda, orienting radio and television shows to this end, as well as publishing houses, theatres and cinemas, opera, ballet, artists' unions, promoting a "militant, revolutionary" character in artistic productions. The liberalisation of 1965 was condemned and an Index of banned books and authors was re-established.

The Theses heralded the beginning of a "mini cultural revolution" in Romania, launching a Neo-Stalinist offensive against cultural autonomy, reaffirming an ideological basis for literature that, in theory, the Party had hardly abandoned. Although presented in terms of "Socialist Humanism", the Theses in fact marked a return to the strict guidelines of Socialist Realism, and attacks on non-compliant intellectuals. Strict ideological conformity in the humanities and social sciences was demanded. Competence and aesthetics were to be replaced by ideology; professionals were to be replaced by agitators; and culture was once again to become an instrument for political-ideological propaganda.

Pacepa defection

In 1978, Ion Mihai Pacepa, a senior member of the Romanian political police (Securitate), defected to the United States. A 2-star general, he was the highest ranking defector from the Eastern Bloc in the history of the Cold War. His defection was a powerful blow against the regime, forcing Ceauşescu to overhaul the architecture of the Securitate. Pacepa's 1986 book, *Red Horizons: Chronicles of a Communist Spy Chief* (ISBN 0895265702), claims to expose details of Ceauşescu's regime, such as collaboration with Arab terrorists, massive espionage on American industry and elaborate efforts to rally Western political support. After Pacepa's defection, the country became more isolated and economic growth faltered. Ceauşescu's intelligence agency became subject to heavy infiltration by foreign intelligence agencies and he started to lose control of the country. He tried several reorganizations in a bid to get rid of old collaborators of Pacepa, but to no avail.

Ceauşescu with East German Leader Erich Honecker in East Berlin

Foreign debt

Despite his increasingly totalitarian rule, Ceauşescu's political independence from the Soviet Union and his protests against the invasion of Czechoslovakia in 1968 drew the interest of Western powers, who briefly believed he was an anti-Soviet maverick and hoped to create a schism in the Warsaw Pact by funding him. Ceauşescu did not realise that the funding was not always very favorable. Ceauşescu was able to borrow heavily (more than $13 billion) from the West to finance economic development programs, but these loans ultimately devastated the country's financial situation. In an attempt to correct this situation, Ceauşescu decided to eradicate Romania's foreign debts. He organised a referendum and managed to change the constitution, adding a clause that barred Romania from taking foreign debts in the future. The referendum yielded a nearly unanimous "yes" vote.

A propaganda poster on the streets of Bucharest, 1986

In the 1980s, Ceauşescu ordered the export of much of the country's agricultural and industrial production in order to repay its debts. The resulting domestic shortages made the everyday life of Romanian citizens a fight for survival as food rationing was introduced and heating, gas and electricity black-outs became the rule. During the 1980s, there was a steady decrease in the living standard, especially the availability and quality of food and general goods in stores. The official explanation was that the country was paying its debts and people accepted the suffering, believing it to be for a short time only and for the ultimate good.

The debt was fully paid in summer 1989, shortly before Ceauşescu was overthrown, but heavy exports continued until the → revolution, which took place in December.

Tensions

By 1989, Ceauşescu was showing signs of complete denial of reality. While the country was going through extremely difficult times with long bread queues in front of empty food shops, he was often shown on state TV entering stores filled with food supplies, visiting large food and arts festivals where people would serve him mouthwatering food while praising the "high living standard" achieved under his rule. Special contingents of food deliveries would fill stores before his visits, and even well-fed cows would be transported across country in anticipation of his visits to farms. Staples such as flour, eggs, butter and milk were difficult to find and most people started to depend on small gardens grown either in small city alleys or out in the country. In late 1989, daily TV broadcasts showed lists of CAPs (kolkhozes) with alleged record harvests, in blatant contradiction to the shortages experienced by the average Romanian at the time.

Stamp commemorating the 70th birthday of Nicolae Ceauşescu, 1988

Some people, believing that Ceauşescu was not aware of what was going on in the country, attempted to hand him petitions and complaint letters during his many visits around the country. However, each time he got a letter, he would immediately pass it on to members of his security. Whether or not Ceauşescu ever read any of them will probably remain unknown. According to rumours of the time,Wikipedia:Avoid weasel words people attempting to hand letters directly to Ceauşescu risked adverse consequences, courtesy of the secret police Securitate. People were strongly discouraged from addressing him and there was a general sense that things had reached an overall low.

Revolution

Main article: → Romanian Revolution of 1989

Ceauşescu's regime collapsed after a series of violent events in Timişoara and Bucharest in December 1989. In November 1989, the XIVth Congress of the Romanian Communist Party (PCR) saw Ceauşescu, then aged 71, re-elected for another 5 years as leader of the PCR.

Timişoara

Demonstrations in the city of Timişoara were triggered by the government-sponsored attempt to evict Laszlo Tokes, an ethnic Hungarian pastor, accused by the government of inciting ethnic hatred. Members of his ethnic Hungarian congregation surrounded his apartment in a show of support.

Romanian students spontaneously joined the demonstration, which soon lost nearly all connection to its initial cause and became a more general anti-government demonstration. Regular military forces, police and Securitate fired on demonstrators on December 17, 1989. On December 18, 1989, Ceauşescu departed for a visit to Iran, leaving the

Nicolae Ceauşescu flees Bucharest by helicopter on December 22, 1989

duty of crushing the Timişoara revolt to his subordinates and his wife. Upon his return on the evening of December 20, the situation became even more tense, and he gave a televised speech from the TV studio inside Central Committee Building (CC Building), in which he spoke about the events at Timişoara in terms of an "interference of foreign forces in Romania's internal affairs" and an "external aggression on Romania's sovereignty".

The country, which had no information of the Timişoara events from the national media, heard about the Timişoara revolt from western radio stations like Voice of America and Radio Free Europe and by word of mouth. A mass meeting was staged for the next day, December 21, which, according to the official media, was presented as a "spontaneous movement of support for Ceauşescu", emulating the 1968 meeting in which Ceauşescu had spoken against the invasion of Czechoslovakia by the Warsaw Pact forces.

Overthrow

On December 21, the mass meeting, held in what is now Revolution Square, degenerated into chaos. The image of Ceauşescu's uncomprehending expression as the crowd began to boo him remains one of the defining moments of the collapse of Communism in Eastern Europe. The stunned couple (the dictator had been joined by his wife), failing to control the crowds, finally took cover inside the building, where they remained until the next day. The rest of the day saw a revolt of the Bucharest population, which had assembled in University Square and confronted the police and the army on barricades. These initial events are regarded to this day as the genuine revolution. However, the unarmed rioters were no match for the military apparatus concentrated in Bucharest, which cleared the streets by midnight and arrested hundreds of people in the process.

Although the broadcast of the "support meeting" and the subsequent events on national television had been interrupted the previous day, Ceauşescu's reaction to the events had already become part of the country's collective memory. By the morning of December 22, the rebellion had already spread to all major cities. The suspicious death of Vasile Milea, the defence minister, was announced by the media. Immediately thereafter, Ceauşescu presided over the CPEX meeting and assumed the leadership of the army. He made an attempt to address the crowd gathered in front of the Central Committee building, but this desperate move was rejected by the rioters, who forced open the doors of the building, by now left unprotected. The Ceauşescus fled by helicopter as the result of a poorly advised decision (since they would have had safer refuge using existing underground tunnels) [see Dumitru Burlan].

During the course of the revolution the western press published estimates of the numbers of people killed by the Securitate in support of Ceauşescu. The numbers increased rapidly until an estimate of 64,000 dead was widely reported and blazoned across front pages. The Hungarian military attache expressed doubt about the figures, pointing out the improbable logistics which would be necessary to kill such a large number of people in such a short time. After Ceauşescu's death a count of the casualties reported at hospitals across the country revealed that the actual death toll had been less than one thousand and probably much lower than that.[7]

Execution

Ceauşescu and his wife Elena fled the capital with Emil Bobu and Manea Mănescu and headed, by helicopter, for Ceauşescu's Snagov residence, from where they fled again, this time for Târgovişte. Near Târgovişte, they abandoned the helicopter, having been ordered to land by the army, which by that time had restricted flying in Romania's air space. The Ceauşescus were held by the police, while the policemen listened to the radio. The police eventually turned over the couple to the army. On Christmas Day, December 25, the two were sentenced to death by a military court on charges ranging from illegal gathering of wealth to genocide, and were executed in Târgovişte. The film crew recording the events missed the execution since the firing began too quickly.[8]

Nicolae Ceauşescu's grave in Ghencea cemetery

The Ceauşescus were executed by a firing squad, which reportedly hundreds volunteered for, consisting of elite paratroop regiment soldiers Ionel Boeru, Dorin Cârlan and Octavian Gheorghiu who shot them with rifles. The firing squad didn't bother to wait for them to be tied up and blindfolded, as is traditional for people to be executed in such a manner, but simply began shooting as soon as they appeared. After the shooting had stopped, the bodies were covered with canvas. The hasty trial and the images of the dead Ceauşescus were videotaped and the footage promptly released in numerous western countries. Footage of their trial and pictures of their corpses (but not of the execution itself) were shown the same day on television for the Romanian public.[9] [10]

The Ceauşescu couple's graves are located in Ghencea cemetery in Bucharest. Nicolae and Elena are buried on opposite sides of a path. The graves themselves are unassuming, but they tend to be covered in flowers and symbols of their regime. Some allege that the graves do not, in reality, contain their bodies. As of April 2007, their son Valentin has lost a lawsuit asking for investigation of the matter. The elder son Nicu Ceauşescu, died in 1996, and is buried close by in the same cemetery. According to *Jurnalul Naţional*,[11] requests were made by their daughter and supporters of their political views to move them to mausoleums or churches built for the purpose of housing their remains, but such requests were denied by the government.

Personality cult and authoritarianism

Ceauşescu created a pervasive personality cult, giving himself the titles of "Conducător" ("Leader") and "Geniul din Carpaţi" ("The Genius of the Carpathians"), with help from Proletarian Culture (Proletkult) poets such as Adrian Păunescu and Corneliu Vadim Tudor, and even had a king-like sceptre made for himself. Such excesses prompted the painter Salvador Dalı to send a congratulatory telegram to the "Conducător." The Communist Party daily *Scînteia* published the message, unaware that it was a work of satire. To avoid new treasons after Pacepa's defection, Ceauşescu also invested his wife Elena and other members of his family with important positions in the government.

Statesmanship

Ceauşescu made efforts to act as a mediator between the PLO and Israel. He organised a successful referendum for reducing the size of the Romanian Army by 5% and held large rallies for peace.

With Warsaw Pact leaders, 1987 (from left): Husak of Czechoslovakia, Zhivkov of Bulgaria, Honecker of East Germany, Gorbachev of the USSR, Ceauşescu, Jaruzelski of Poland, and Kadar of Hungary

Ceauşescu tried to play a role of influence and guidance to South American countries. He was a close ally and personal friend of dictator President Mobutu Sese Seko of Zaïre. Relations were in fact not just state-to-state, but party-to-party between the MPR and the Romanian Communist Party. Many believe that Ceauşescu's death played a role in influencing Mobutu to "democratize" Zaïre in 1990.[12] Also, France granted Ceauşescu the Legion of Honour and in 1978 he became an Honorary British Knight[13] (GCB, removed) in the UK, whereas the illiterate Elena Ceauşescu was arranged to be 'elected' to membership of a Science Academy in the USA; all of these, and more, were arranged by the Ceauşescus as a propaganda ploy through the consular cultural attaches of Romanian embassies in the countries involved.

Ceauşescu's Romania was the only Warsaw Pact country that did not sever diplomatic relations with Chile after Augusto Pinochet's coup.[14]

Weaknesses

Ceauşescu's control of every aspect of religious, educational, commercial, social, and civic life[15] further aggravated the situation. In 1987, an attempted strike at Braşov failed: the army occupied the factories and crushed the workers' demonstrations.

Throughout 1989, Ceauşescu became ever more isolated in the Communist world. In August 1989, he proposed a summit to discuss the problems of Eastern European Communism and defend socialism in these countries, but his proposal was turned down by the Warsaw Pact states and the People's Republic of China. Even after the fall of the Berlin Wall and the downfall of Ceauşescu's close comrades GDR leader Eric Honecker, who resigned, and Bulgarian leader Todor Zhivkov, who was replaced in November 1989, Ceauşescu ignored the threat to his position as the last old-style Communist leader in Eastern Europe.

Other

Nicolae and Elena Ceauşescu had three children, Valentin Ceauşescu (born 1948) a nuclear physicist, Nicu Ceauşescu (1951 - 1996) also a physicist, and a daughter Zoia Ceauşescu (1949 - 2006), who was a mathematician. After the death of his parents, Nicolae Ceauşescu ordered the construction of an Orthodox church, the walls of which are decorated with portraits of his parents.[11]

Ceauşescu is the only recipient of the Danish Order of the Elephant ever to have it revoked. This happened on December 23, 1989, when HM Queen Margrethe II ordered the insignia to be returned to Denmark, and for Ceauşescu's name to be deleted from the official records.

His successor, Ion Iliescu, and Nicolae Ceauşescu in 1976

Ceauşescu was likewise stripped of his honorary GCB (Knight, Grand Cross of the Bath) by Queen Elizabeth II of the United Kingdom on the day before his execution. Queen Elizabeth also returned the Romanian Order Ceauşescu had bestowed upon her.[16]

On his 70th birthday in 1988 Ceauşescu was decorated with the Karl-Marx-Orden by then Socialist Unity Party of Germany (SED) chief Erich Honecker; through this he was honoured for his rejection of Mikhail Gorbachev's reforms.

In a similar way to some EU countries, praising the crimes of totalitarian regimes and denigrating their victims is forbidden by law in Romania; this includes the Ceauşescu regime. Dinel Staicu received a 25,000 lei (approximately 9,000 United States dollars) fine for praising Ceauşescu and displaying his pictures on his private television channel (*3TV Oltenia*).[17]

Ceauşescu's last days in power were dramatized in a stage musical, *The Fall of Ceauşescu*, written and composed by Ron Conner. It premiered at the Los Angeles Theater Center in September 1995 and was attended by Ion Iliescu, the then president of Romania who had been visiting Los Angeles at the time.

"Ceauşism"

While the term *Ceauşism* became widely used inside Romania, usually as a pejorative, it never achieved status in academia. This feature can be explained taking in view the largely crude and syncretic character of the dogma. Ceauşescu attempted the inclusion of his views in mainstream Marxist theory, to which he added his belief in a "multilaterally developed socialist society" as a necessary stage between the Marxist concepts of Socialist and Communist societies (a critical view reveals that the main reason for the interval is the disappearance of the State and Party structures in Communism). A Romanian Encyclopedic Dictionary entry in 1978 underlines the concept as "a new, superior, stage in the socialist development of Romania [...] begun by the 1971-1975 [sic] Five-Year Plan, prolonged over several [succeeding and projected] Five-Year Plans".[18]

The main trait observed was a form of Romanian nationalism,[19] one which arguably propelled Ceauşescu to power in 1965, and probably accounted for the Party leadership that was gathered around Ion Gheorghe Maurer choosing him over the more orthodox Gheorghe Apostol. Although he had previously been a careful supporter of the official lines, Ceauşescu came to embody Romanian society's wish for independence after what were broadly considered to have been years of Soviet directives and purges, during and after the SovRom fiasco. He carried this nationalist option inside the Party, manipulating it against the nominated successor Apostol. This nationalist policy was not without more timid precedent:[20] for example, the Gheorghiu-Dej regime had overseen the withdrawal of the Red Army in 1958.

As well, it had engineered the publishing of several works that were subversive of the Russian and Soviet image, such as the final volumes of the official *History of Romania*, no longer glossing over the traditional points of tension with Russia and the Soviet Union (even alluding to an unlawful Soviet presence in Bessarabia). In the final years of Gheorghiu-Dej's rule more problems were brought out in the open, with the publication of a collection of Karl Marx texts that dealt with Romanian topics, showing Marx's previously-censored, politically uncomfortable views of Russia.

However, Ceauşescu was prepared to take a more decisive step in questioning Soviet policies. In the early years of his rule, he generally relaxed political pressures inside Romanian society,[21] which led to the late 1960s and early 1970s being the most liberal decade in Communist Romania. Gaining the public's confidence, Ceauşescu took a clear stand against the 1968 crushing of the Prague Spring by Leonid Brezhnev. After a visit paid by Charles de Gaulle earlier in the same year (during which the French President gave recognition to the incipient maverick), Ceauşescu's public speech in August deeply impressed the population, not only through its themes, but also by the unique fact that it was unscripted. He immediately attracted Western sympathies and backing, which lasted, out of inertia, beyond the liberal phase of his regime; at the same time, the period brought forward the threat of armed Soviet invasion: significantly, many young men inside Romania joined the *Patriotic Guards* created on the spur of the moment, in order to meet the perceived threat.[22] President Richard Nixon was invited to Bucharest in 1969, which was the first visit of a United States president to a Communist country.

Alexander Dubček's version of *Socialism with a human face* was never suited to Romanian communist goals. Ceauşescu found himself briefly aligned with Dubček's Czechoslovakia and Josip Broz Tito's Socialist Federal Republic of Yugoslavia. The latter friendship was to last well into the 1980s, with Ceauşescu adapting the Titoist doctrine of "independent socialist development" to suit his own objectives. Romania proclaimed itself a "Socialist" (in place of "People's") Republic to show that it was fulfilling Marxist goals without Moscow's overseeing.

The system exacerbated its nationalist traits, which it progressively blended with Juche and Maoist ideals. In 1971, the Party, which had already been completely purged of internal opposition (with the possible exception of Gheorghe Gaston Marin),[20] approved the *July Theses*, expressing Ceauşescu's disdain of Western models as a whole, and the reevaluation of the recent liberalisation as *bourgeois*. The 1974 11th Congress tightened the grip on Romanian culture, guiding it towards Ceauşescu's nationalist principles:[23] notably, Romanian historians were demanded to refer to Dacians as having "an unorganised State [sic]", part of a political continuum that culminated in the Socialist Republic.[23] The regime continued its cultural dialogue with ancient forms, with Ceauşescu connecting his cult of personality to figures such as Mircea cel Bătrân (whom he styled *Mircea the Great*) and Mihai Viteazul; it also started adding Dacian or Roman versions to the names of cities and towns (*Drobeta* to Turnu Severin, *Napoca* to Cluj).[24]

A new generation of committed supporters on the outside confirmed the regime's character. Ceauşescu probably never gave importance to the fact that his policies constituted a paradigm for theorists of National Bolshevism such as Jean-François Thiriart, but there was a publicised connection between him and Iosif Constantin Drăgan, an Iron Guardist Romanian-Italian emigre millionaire (Drăgan was already committed to a Dacian Protochronism that largely echoed the official cultural policy).

Nicolae Ceauşescu had a major influence on modern-day Romanian populist rhetorics. In his final years, he had begun to rehabilitate the image of pro-Nazi dictator Ion Antonescu. Although Antonescu's was never a fully official myth in Ceauşescu's time, today's xenophobic politicians such as Corneliu Vadim Tudor have coupled the images of the two leaders into their versions of a national Pantheon. The conflict with Hungary over the treatment of the Magyar minority in Romania had several unusual aspects: not only was it a vitriolic argument between two officially Socialist states (as Hungary had not yet officially embarked on the course to a free market economy), it also marked the moment when Hungary, a state behind the Iron Curtain, appealed to the Organisation for Security and Co-operation in Europe for sanctions to be taken against Romania. This meant that the later 1980s were marked by a pronounced anti-Hungarian discourse, which owed more to nationalist tradition than Marxism,[25] and the ultimate isolation of Romania on the World stage.

The strong opposition of his regime to all forms of *perestroika* and *glasnost* placed Ceauşescu at odds with Mikhail Gorbachev. In a dramatic twist, Ceauşescu demanded that the Soviet leadership return to its previous stance, even asking for a Soviet crackdown on all Eastern Bloc liberation movements in the second half of 1989.

In November 1989, at the XIVth and last congress of the PCR, Ceauşescu condemned the Molotov-Ribbentrop Pact and asked for the annulment of its consequences. In effect, this amounted to claiming back Bessarabia (most of which was then a Soviet republic and since 1991 has been an independent state) and northern Bukovina, both of which had been occupied by the Soviet Union in 1940 and again at the end of World War II.

Selected published works

- *Report during the joint solemn session of the CC of the Romanian Communist Party, the National Council of the Socialist Unity Front and the Grand National Assembly: Marking the 60th anniversary of the creation of a Unitary Romanian National State*, 1978
- *Major problems of our time: Eliminating underdevelopment, bridging gaps between states, building a new international economic order*, 1980
- *The solving of the national question in Romania (Socio-political thought of Romania's President)*, 1980
- *Ceauşescu: Builder of Modern Romania and International Statesman*, 1983
- *The nation and co-habiting nationalities in the contemporary epoch (Philosophical thought of Romania's president)*, 1983
- *Istoria poporului Român în concepţia preşedintelui*, 1988

References

- *Mic Dicţionar Enciclopedic* ("Small encyclopedic dictionary"), 1978
- Edward Behr, *Kiss the Hand you Cannot Bite*, ISBN 0679401288
- Dumitru Burlan, *Dupa 14 ani - Sosia lui Ceauşescu se destăinuie* ("After 14 Years - The Double of Ceauşescu confesses"). Editura Ergorom. July 31, 2003 (in Romanian).
- Juliana Geran Pilon, *The Bloody Flag. Post-Communist Nationalism in Eastern Europe. Spotlight on Romania*, ISBN 1-56000-062-7; ISBN 1-56000-620-X
- Marian Oprea, "Au trecut 15 ani -- Conspiraţia Securităţii" ("After 15 years -- the conspiracy of Securitate"), in *Lumea Magazin* Nr 10, 2004 [9]: (in Romanian; link leads to table of contents, verifying that the article exists, but the article itself is not online).
- Viorel Patrichi, "Eu am fost sosia lui Nicolae Ceauşescu [8]" ("I was Ceauşescu's double"), *Lumea Magazin* Nr 12, 2001 (in Romanian)
- Stevens W. Sowards, *Twenty-Five Lectures on Modern Balkan History (The Balkans in the Age of Nationalism)* [26], 1996, in particular Lecture 24: The failure of Balkan Communism and the causes of the Revolutions of 1989 [27]
- Victor Stănculescu, "Nu vă fie milă, au 2 miliarde de lei în cont" [28] ("Do not have mercy, they hold 2 billion lei [33 million dollars] in their account[s]"), in *Jurnalul Naţional*, Nov 22, 2004
- John Sweeney, *The Life and Evil Times of Nicolae Ceauşescu*, ISBN 0091746728
- Stelian Tănase, "Societatea civilă românească şi violenţa" ("Romanian Civil Society and Violence"), in *Agora*, issue 3/IV, July-September 1991
- Filip Teodorescu, et al., Extracts from the minutes of a Romanian senate hearing, 14 December 1994, featuring the remarks of Filip Teodorescu.

External links

- Ceauşescu, Nicolae - Romania under Communism [10]
  - Nicolae Ceauşescu's last speech in public [15]
  - Ceauşescu's trial transcripts (in English) [29]
  - Ceauşescu's trial transcripts (in Romanian) [30]
- Communist Romania's Demographic Policy [31]
- The Politicians and the revolution of 1989 [32]
- Gheorghe Brătescu, *Clipa* 638: Un complot ratat [33] ("A failed scheme"). On how Milea died, probably killed by Stănculescu according to this writer, and the life of the Ceauşescu family. (In Romanian)
- Death of the Father: Nicolae Ceauşescu [34] Focuses on his death, but also discusses other matters. Many photos.

- "Killer File" entry on Nicolae Andruţa Ceauşescu [35] Chronological overview of important events in his life and rule.

Preceded by **Gheorghe Gheorghiu-Dej**	**General secretary** of the Romanian Communist Party**1965–1989**	Succeeded by **none; party dissolved**

References

[1] Johanna Granville, "*Dej*-a-Vu: Early Roots of Romania's Independence," (http://www.scribd.com/doc/17679545/ DejAVu-Early-Roots-of-Romanias-Independence-by-Johanna-Granville) *East European Quarterly*, vol. XLII, no. 4 (Winter 2008), pp. 365-404.

[2] Jeri Laber The Courage of Strangers (http://books.google.com/books?id=eeCT2svkPIYC&pg=RA1-PA340&dq=kangaroo+court+romania)

[3] Ceausescu.org (http://www.ceausescu.org/ceausescu_texts/ceausescu_chronology.htm)

[4] Communist Romania's Demographic Policy, U.S. Library of Congress country study (http://www.country-studies.com/romania/demographic-policy.html)for details see Gail Kligman. 1998. *The Politics of Duplicity. Controlling Reproduction in Ceausescu's Romania*. Berkeley: University of California Press.

[5] Ceausescu's Longest-Lasting Legacy - the Cohort of '67 (http://www.sustainabilityinstitute.org/dhm_archive/index. php?display_article=vn318cohort_of67ed)

[6] See, for instance, Bohlen, Celestine, In 1966, the first abortion law was passed which declared abortion in that country, illegal. This law was followed by other measures which ensured compliance with the law. These include financial advantages for families who bear children, guaranteed maternity leave, and childcare support for mothers returning to work, work protection for women, and extensive access to medical control in all stages of pregnancy, as well as after. Medical control is seen as one of the most productive effects of the law, since all women who became pregnant were under the care of a qualified medical practitioner, even in rural areas. In some cases, if the women was unable to attend a medical office, the doctor would make visits to her home. "Upheaval in the East: Romania's AIDS Babies: A Legacy of Neglect," (http://query.nytimes.com/gst/fullpage.html?sec=health&res=9C0CE5DA103AF93BA35751C0A966958260) February 8, 1990, in *The New York Times*.

[7] Aubin, Stephen P (1998). *Distorting defense: network news and national security* (http://books.google.com/books?id=5YH5rPgWvzUC& pg=PA158&dq=revolution+romania+1989+death+toll&lr=&as_drrb_is=q&as_minm_is=0&as_miny_is=&as_maxm_is=0& as_maxy_is=&as_brr=3). Greenwood Publishing Group. pp. 158. ISBN 9780275963033. . Retrieved 28/June/2008.

[8] George Galloway and Bob Wylie, *Downfall: The Ceausescus and the Romanian Revolution* p. 198-199. Futura Publications, 1991

[9] Daniel Simpson, "Ghosts of Christmas past still haunt Romanians" (http://danielsimpson.blogspot.com/ 2001_12_01_danielsimpson_archive.html)

[10] The dictator and his henchman (http://translate.google.com/translate?u=http://www.stern.de/politik/ausland/ :Ceausescus-Scharfrichter-Der-Diktator-Henker/547930.html&hl=en&ie=UTF8&sl=de&tl=en)

[11] *Jurnalul Naţional*, January 25, 2005

[12] Relations with the Communist World (http://lcweb2.loc.gov/cgi-bin/query/r?frd/cstdy:@field(DOCID+zr0173)) Library of Congress Country Study on Zaire (Former), Library of Congress Call Number DT644 .Z3425 1994. (TOC (http://lcweb2.loc.gov/frd/cs/zrtoc. html#zr0173).) Data as of December 1993. Accessed online October 15, 2006.

[13] List of honorary British Knights

[14] Valenzuela, J. Samuel and Arturo Valenzuela (eds.), *Military Rule in Chile: Dictatorship and Oppositions*, p. 321

[15] Tănase, p.24-25

[16] The Official Website of the British Monarchy: *Queen and Public - Honours* (http://www.royal.gov.uk/output/Page4872.asp), retrieved on 2008-01-04.

[17] Official communique of the National Board of the Audio-Visual, originally at www.cna.ro/comunicare/comunic/2006/c0207.html but now removed, accessible through web.archive.org (http://web.archive.org/web/20071220071037/http://www.cna.ro/comunicare/comunic/ 2006/c0207.html)

[18] *Mic Dicţionar Enciclopedic*

[19] Geran Pilon, Chapter III, *Communism with a Nationalist Face*, p.60-66; Tănase, p.24

[20] Geran Pilon, p.60

[21] Tănase, p.23

[22] Geran Pilon, p.62

[23] Geran Pilon, p.61

[24] Geran Pilon, p.61-63

[25] Geran Pilon, p.63

History of Romania since 1989

History of Romania
This article is part of **a series**
Prehistory
Dacia
Dacian Wars
Roman Dacia
Thraco-Roman
Early Middle Ages
Origin of the Romanians
Middle Ages
History of Transylvania
Principality of Transylvania
Foundation of Wallachia
Foundation of Moldavia
Early Modern Times
Phanariotes
National awakening
Organic Statute
1848 Moldavian Revolution
1848 Wallachian Revolution
United Principalities
War of Independence
Kingdom of Romania
World War I
Greater Romania
World War II
Soviet occupation of Bessarabia and Northern Bukovina
→ **Communist Romania**
Soviet occupation
→ 1989 Revolution
→ **Romania since 1989**
Topic
Timeline

Military history
Romania Portal

1989 revolution

Main article: → Romanian Revolution of 1989

1989 marked the fall of Communism in Eastern Europe. A mid-December protest in Timişoara against the eviction of a Hungarian minister (Laszlo Tokes) grew into a country-wide protest against the Ceauşescu regime, sweeping the dictator from power.

On December 22, President → Nicolae Ceauşescu had his apparatus gather a mass-meeting in Bucharest downtown in an attempt to rally popular support for his regime and publicly condemn the mass protests of Timişoara. This meeting mirrored the mass-meeting gathered in 1968 when Ceauşescu had spoken out against the invasion of Czechoslovakia by the Warsaw Treaty countries. This time however, the people turned angry and riot broke out. During the events of the following week, marked by confusion and street fighting, it is estimated that 1,051 people lost their lives. To this day, the real number of casualties are unknown and so are the identities of the individuals responsible for them. Those responsible for the casualties are still called "the terrorists". Ceauşescu was arrested in Târgovişte. After a summary trial by a kangaroo court, he and his wife were executed on December 25.

During the → Romanian Revolution of 1989, power was taken by a group called the National Salvation Front (FSN), which grouped a large number of former members of the Communist Party and Securitate (the Romanian equivalent of the KGB) but also a small number of dissidents and other participants in the uprising who genuinely thought the FSN to be an anti-Communist movement. The FSN quickly assumed the mission of restoring civil order and immediately took seemingly democratic measures. The Communist Party was thus outlawed, and Ceauşescu's most unpopular measures, such as bans on abortion and contraception, were rolled back.

1990 - 1996

See also: Ethnic clashes of Târgu Mureş, Golaniad, and Mineriad

Despite the efforts of the State media (entirely controlled by the FSN) to hide the pro-Communist and pro-regime history of FSN members, public opinion regarded it as being a new name of the Romanian Communist Party. This triggered a series of anti-communist demonstrations in Bucharest and the resurrection of traditional parties that were once the main parties in Romania before being outlawed. These traditional parties are the National Christian Democrat Peasant's Party (PNȚCD), the revived form of which is today's Christian-Democratic National Peasants' Party; the National Liberal Party (PNL) revived under the same name; and (in 1992) the Romanian Social Democrat Party (PSDR), the revived form of which is today's Social

Romanian flag with a hole in the center, as → used in 1989; photo made during an anti-government demonstration in Bucharest in September 2006

Democratic Party, all of whom were led by non-communists and former political prisoners of the Communist regime. These parties rallied a great amount of public support in a very short time despite the FSN's directed efforts to discredit their leaders by spreading what are now known to be lies and false rumors through the State controlled media. Their rapidly rising popularity raised concern among FSN leaders who feared losing power and thus having to answer for the crimes committed during the Ceauşescu regime. Ion Iliescu, leader of FSN, called the miners in to Bucharest several times and directed them to repress the opposition demonstrations.[1] [2] [3] [4] [5] [6] [7] ; these incidents are remembered as the Mineriads.

On February 28, less than a month after the Mineriad, another anti-Communist demonstration in Bucharest ended again with a confrontation between demonstrators and coal miners. This time, despite the demonstrators' pleas for non-violence, several people started throwing stones at the Government building. Riot police and army forces intervened to restore order, and on the same night, 4,000 miners rushed into Bucharest. This incident is known as the Mineriad of February 1990. There are suspicions [8] that these events were manipulated by the new Secret Services, composed of the remnants of the Securitate which had conserved its infrastructure and its network of agents among the people.

Presidential and parliamentary elections were held on May 20, 1990. Iliescu won with almost 90% of the popular vote and thus became the first elected President of Romania. The FSN also secured more than two-thirds of the seats in Parliament. Petre Roman, a professor at the Polytechnic University of Bucharest and a person with strong family roots in the Communist Party, was named Prime Minister. The new government, largely composed of former Communist officials and former members of the Securitate, promised the implementation of some free market reforms.

The results of these elections prompted further anti-Communist demonstrations, called Golaniad by FSN leaders, which ended in yet another brutal Mineriad. It began when a sit-in demonstration against the FSN in University Square grew into a continuing mass demonstration. Protesters were contesting the results of the recently held elections and accusing the FSN of being made up of former Communists and Securitate members. These demonstrations (which had been peaceful) degenerated when the police attacked hunger strikers and the Architecture Institute where students had taken refuge. Events of 13 June led to a police bus being incinerated. This incident is believed to have been fabricated by former Securitate members in order to justify the use of force against protesters. The implication of secret service in these events was later acknowledged by the Serviciul Român de Informaţii (SRI, Romanian Intelligence Service) in an open letter to the Romanian parliament sent by SRI captain Adrian Ionescu. At Iliescu's request[9] , thousands of miners from the Jiu Valley descended on Bucharest under the command of their trade union leader Miron Cozma. The miners, some of them wielding wooden clubs, axes and other make-shift weapons, confronted the demonstrators and forcefully cleared University Square. Miners claimed that most of the violence was perpetuated by individuals hired by the government and who were dressed as miners. After clearing the Square of demonstrators, some of the groups shifted their focus and assaulted the headquarters of the opposition parties as well as the private residences of the opposition leaders. President Iliescu publicly thanked the miners for their help with restoring the order in Bucharest. This episode is remembered as the June 1990 Mineriad.

In December 1991, a new constitution was drafted and subsequently adopted, after a popular referendum. March 1992 marked the split of the FSN into two groups: the Democratic National Salvation Front (FDSN), led by Ion Iliescu and the Democrat Party (PD), led by Petre Roman. Iliescu won the presidential elections in September 1992 by a clear margin, and his FDSN won the general elections held at the same time. With parliamentary support from the nationalist National Unity Party of Romanians (PUNR), Greater Romania Party (PRM), and the ex-communist Socialist Workers' Party

Romania in 2008

(PSM), a new government was formed in November 1992 under Prime Minister Nicolae Văcăroiu, an economist and former Communist Party official. The FDSN changed its name to Party of Social Democracy in Romania (PDSR) in July 1993. The Văcăroiu government ruled in coalition with three smaller parties. This coalition dissolved before the November 1996 elections. This coincided with the bankruptcy of the Caritas pyramid scheme, a major scandal at the time in Romania.

1996 - 2000

Emil Constantinescu of the Democrat Convention of Romania (CDR) won the second round of the 1996 presidential elections by a comfortable margin of 9% and thus replaced Iliescu as chief of state. (see: Romanian election, 1996)

PDSR won the largest number of seats in Parliament, but was unable to form a viable coalition. Constituent parties of the CDR joined the Democratic Party (PD), the National Liberal Party (PNL) and the Hungarian Democratic Union of Romania (UDMR) to form a centrist coalition government, holding 60% of the seats in Parliament. This coalition of sorts frequently struggled for survival, as decisions were often delayed by long periods of negotiations among the involved parties. Nevertheless, this coalition was able to implement several critical reforms. The new coalition government, under prime minister Victor Ciorbea remained in office until March 1998, when Radu Vasile (PNTCD) took over as prime minister. The former governor of the National Bank, Mugur Isărescu, eventually replaced Radu Vasile as head of the government.

2000 - 2004

Iliescu's Social Democratic Party, now renamed the Party of Social Democracy in Romania (PDSR), returned to power in the 2000 elections, and Iliescu won a third term as the country's president. Adrian Năstase became the Prime Minister of the newly formed government. His rule was shaken by recurring allegations of corruption.

2004 - 2007

See also: Accession of Romania to the European Union

Presidential and parliamentary elections took place again on November 28, 2004. No political party was able to secure a viable parliamentary majority. There was no winner in the first round of the presidential elections. Finally, the joint PNL-PD candidate, Traian Băsescu, won the second round on December 12, 2004 with 51% of the vote and thus became the third post-revolutionary president of Romania.

The PNL leader, Călin Popescu-Tăriceanu, was assigned the difficult task of building a coalition government excluding the PSD. In December 2004, the new coalition government (PD, PNL, PUR (Romanian Humanist Party) and UDMR) under prime minister Tăriceanu was sworn in.

Romania joined the North Atlantic Treaty Organization (NATO) in 2004, and the European Union (EU), alongside Bulgaria, on January 1, 2007.

After 2007

Main article: Romanian membership of the European Union

See also

• Romanian property bubble

References

[1] YouTube - Piata Universitatii 13-15 iunie [3] (http://www.youtube.com/watch?v=b-zD-fUsXa8)
[2] http://www.onlinenews.ro/detaliere.php?id=257175
[3] Editie Speciala de Oltenia - un ziar european (http://www.editie.ro/mod.php?mod=stiri&idstire=27710)
[4] Gardianul: La mitingul partidelor istorice, FSN a raspuns cu o manifestatie stalinista (http://web.archive.org/web/20040309221137/http:/
      /www.gardianul.ro/print.php?a=reportaj2004012901.xml)
[5] http://www.edrc.ro/docs/docs/cartea-alba05.pdf
[6] Andreescu.p65 (http://www.edrc.ro/docs/docs/ruleta.pdf)
[7] ZIUA pe Internet (http://www.ziua.ro/prt.php?id=184871&data=2005-09-17&ziua=87a88c6955e5b8f2f093d438a8a267fe)
[8] "Mostenitorii Securitatii" Marius Oprea
[9] http://www.avmr.ro/media/Mineriada_Iliescu_1-4.avi

Revolutions of 1989

"Fall of Communism" redirects here. For the fall of the Soviet Union itself, see History of the Soviet Union (1985–1991).

The **Revolutions of 1989**, sometimes called the **Autumn of Nations**,[1] , were a revolutionary wave that swept across Central and Eastern Europe in late 1989, ending in the overthrow of Soviet-style communist states within the space of a few months.[2]

The largely bloodless political upheaval began in Poland,[3] [4] continued in Hungary, and then led to a surge of mostly peaceful revolutions in East Germany, Czechoslovakia, and Bulgaria. → Romania was the only Eastern-bloc country to overthrow its communist regime violently and execute its head of state.[5] The subsequent events that continued in 1990 and 1991 are sometimes also referred to as a part of the revolutions of 1989. The Soviet Union collapsed by the end of 1991.

The Revolutions of 1989 greatly altered the balance of power in the world and marked the end of the Cold War and the beginning of the Post-Cold War era.

Territory of former Eastern Bloc states with the dates that Communist rule ended

The advent of "new thinking"

Although several Eastern bloc countries had attempted some abortive, limited economic and political reform since the 1950s (Hungarian Revolution of 1956, Prague Spring of 1968), the advent of reform-minded Soviet leader Mikhail Gorbachev in 1985 signaled the trend toward greater liberalization. During the mid 1980s, a younger generation of Soviet apparatchiks, led by Gorbachev, began advocating fundamental reform in order to reverse years of Brezhnev stagnation. The Soviet Union was facing a period of severe economic decline and needed Western technology and credits to make up for its increasing backwardness. The costs of maintaining its so-called "empire" — the military, KGB, subsidies to foreign client states — further strained the moribund Soviet economy.

Ronald Reagan at the Berlin Wall, June 1987: "Tear down this wall!"

The first signs of major reform came in 1986 when Gorbachev launched a policy of *glasnost* (openness) in the Soviet Union, and emphasized the need for *perestroika* (economic restructuring). By the spring of 1989, the Soviet Union had not only experienced lively media debate, but had also held its first multi-candidate elections in the newly established Congress of People's Deputies. Though glasnost advocated openness and political criticism, at the time, it was only permitted in accordance with the political views of the Communists. The general public in the Eastern bloc were still threatened by secret police and political repression.

From East to West

Moscow's largest obstacle to improved political and economic relations with the Western powers remained the Iron Curtain that existed between East and West. As long as the specter of Soviet military intervention loomed over Eastern Europe, it seemed unlikely that Moscow could attract the Western economic support needed to finance the country's restructuring. Gorbachev urged his Eastern European counterparts to imitate *perestroika* and *glasnost* in their own countries. However, while reformists in Hungary and Poland were emboldened by the force of liberalization spreading from East to West, other Eastern bloc countries remained openly skeptical and demonstrated aversion to reform. Past experiences had demonstrated that although reform in the Soviet Union was manageable, the pressure for change in Eastern Europe had the potential to become uncontrollable. These regimes owed their creation and continued survival to Soviet-style authoritarianism, backed by Soviet military power and subsidies. Believing Gorbachev's reform initiatives would be short-lived, orthodox Communist rulers like East Germany's Erich Honecker, Bulgaria's Todor Zhivkov, Czechoslovakia's Gustav Husak, and → Romania's → Nicolae Ceauşescu obstinately ignored the calls for change.[6] "When your neighbor puts up new wallpaper, it doesn't mean you have to too," declared one East German politburo member.[7]

Political alignment of European states before the Revolutions of 1989.
Blue: Western bloc states
Light blue: Non-NATO liberal democracies.
Red: Warsaw Pact member states
Pink: Non-Warsaw Pact socialist states
Black line: the Iron Curtain

Gorbachev's visit to the People's Republic of China on May 15 during the Tiananmen Square Protests of 1989, brought many foreign news agencies to Beijing, and their sympathetic portrayals of the protesters helped galvanize a spirit of liberation among the Eastern Europeans who were watching. The Chinese leadership, particularly Communist Party General Secretary Zhao Ziyang, having begun earlier than the Soviets to radically reform the economy, was open to political reform, but not at the cost of a potential return to the disorder of the Cultural Revolution.

Eastern Bloc collapse

Reform in Poland

Main article: End of Communism in Poland (1989)

By 1989, the Soviet Union had repealed the Brezhnev Doctrine in favor of non-intervention in the internal affairs of its Warsaw Pact allies, termed the Sinatra Doctrine in a joking reference to the song "My Way". Poland became the first Warsaw Pact state country to break free of Soviet domination. Taking notice from Poland, Hungary was next to follow.

Lech Wałęsa

Labour turmoil in Poland during 1980 had led to the formation of the independent trade union, Solidarity, led by Lech Wałęsa, which over time became a political force. On December 13, 1981, Communist leader Wojciech Jaruzelski started a crack-down on Solidarity, declaring martial law in Poland, suspending the union, and temporarily imprisoning all of its leaders. Throughout the mid-1980s, Solidarity persisted solely as an underground organization, supported by the Catholic Church. However, by the late 1980s, Solidarity became sufficiently strong to frustrate Jaruzelski's attempts at reform, and nationwide strikes in 1988 forced the government to open a dialogue with Solidarity. On March 9, 1989, both sides agreed to a bicameral legislature called the National Assembly. The already existing Sejm would become the lower house. The Senate would be elected by the people. Traditionally a ceremonial office, the presidency was given more powers[8] (Polish Round Table Agreement).

In April 1989, Solidarity was again legalized and allowed to participate in parliamentary elections on June 4, 1989 (incidentally, the day following the midnight crackdown on Chinese protesters in Tiananmen Square). A political earthquake followed. The victory of Solidarity surpassed all predictions. Solidarity candidates captured all the seats they were allowed to compete for in the Sejm, while in the Senate they captured 99 out of the 100 available seats (with the one remaining seat taken by an independent candidate). At the same time, many prominent Communist candidates failed to gain even the minimum number of votes required to capture the seats that were reserved for them. A new non-Communist government, the first of its kind in the former Eastern Bloc, was sworn into office in September 1989.

Hungary

Main article: End of Communism in Hungary (1989)

See also: Removal of Hungary's border fence

Following Poland's lead, Hungary was next to revert to a non-communist government. Although Hungary had achieved some lasting economic reforms and limited political liberalization during the 1980s, major reforms only occurred following the replacement of Janos Kadar as General Secretary of the Communist Party in 1988. That same year, the Parliament adopted a "democracy package", which included trade union pluralism; freedom of association, assembly, and the press; a new electoral law; and a radical revision of the constitution, among others.

In October 1989, the Communist Party convened its last congress and re-established itself as the Hungarian Socialist Party, which still exists today (see MSZP). In a historic session from October 16 to October 20, the parliament adopted legislation providing for multi-party parliamentary elections and a direct presidential election. The legislation transformed Hungary from a People's Republic into the

Comrades it's Over! — political poster saying goodbye to Soviet troops in Hungary in 1989

Republic of Hungary, guaranteed human and civil rights, and created an institutional structure that ensured separation of powers among the judicial, legislative, and executive branches of government. Hungarians suggested that Soviet troops "go home" — an idea first suggested by Viktor Orban at the re-burying funeral of Imre Nagy.Wikipedia:Citation needed

Fall of the Berlin Wall

Main articles: Peaceful revolution (German), Die Wende, and German reunification

See also: East Germany, Inner German border, Eastern Bloc emigration and defection, Monday demonstrations in East Germany, Pan-European Picnic, and Fall of the Berlin Wall

Walking through Checkpoint Charlie, 10 November 1989

After a reformed border was opened from Hungary, a growing number of East Germans began emigrating to West Germany via Hungary's border with Austria. By the end of September 1989, more than 30,000 East Germans had escaped to the West before the GDR denied travel to Hungary, leaving the CSSR (Czechoslovakia) as the only neighboring state where East Germans could travel. Thousands of East Germans tried to reach the West by occupying the West German diplomatic facilities in other Eastern European capitals, notably the Prague Embassy where thousands camped in the muddy garden from August to November. The GDR closed the border to the CSSR in early October, thereby isolating itself from all neighbors. Having been shut off from their last chance for escape, East Germans began mass demonstrations. Hundreds of thousands of people in several cities — particularly Leipzig — eventually took part.

On 6 October and 7 October, Gorbachev visited East Germany to mark the 40th anniversary of the German Democratic Republic, and urged the East German leadership to accept reform. A famous quote of his is rendered in German as "Wer zu spät kommt, den bestraft das Leben" (*He who is too late is punished by life*). However, the elderly Erich Honecker remained opposed to internal reform, with his regime even going so far as forbidding the circulation of Soviet publications that it viewed as subversive.

Faced with ongoing civil unrest, the ruling Socialist Unity Party (SED) deposed Honecker in mid-October, and replaced him with Egon Krenz. Also, the border to Czechoslovakia was opened again, but the Czechoslovak authorities soon let all East Germans travel directly to West Germany without further bureaucratic ado, thus lifting their part of the Iron Curtain on 3 November. Unable to stem the ensuing flow of refugees to the West through Czechoslovakia, the East German authorities eventually caved in to public pressure by allowing East German citizens to enter West Berlin and West Germany directly, via existing border points, on November 9, without having properly briefed the border guards. Triggered by the erratic words of Günter Schabowski in a TV press conference, stating that the planned changes were "in effect immediately", hundreds of thousands of people took advantage of the opportunity; soon new crossing points were opened in the Berlin Wall and along the border with West Germany. By December, Krenz had been replaced, and the SED's monopoly on power had ended. This led to the acceleration of the process of reforms in East Germany that ended with the eventual reunification of East and West Germany that came into force on 3 October 1990.

The Kremlin's willingness to abandon such a strategically vital ally marked a dramatic shift by the Soviet superpower and a fundamental paradigm change in international relations, which until 1989 had been dominated by the East-West divide running through Berlin itself.

The Velvet Revolution in Czechoslovakia

Main article: Velvet Revolution

The "Velvet Revolution" was a non-violent revolution in Czechoslovakia that saw the overthrow of the Communist government. On November 17, 1989 (Friday), riot police suppressed a peaceful student demonstration in Prague. That event sparked a series of popular demonstrations from November 19 to late December. By November 20 the number of peaceful protesters assembled in Prague had swelled from 200,000 the previous day to an estimated half-million. A two-hour general strike, involving all citizens of Czechoslovakia, was held on November 27.

With the collapse of other Communist governments, and increasing street protests, the Communist Party of Czechoslovakia announced on November 28 that it would relinquish power and dismantle the single-party state. Barbed wire and other obstructions were removed from the border with West Germany and Austria in early December. On December 10, President Gustav Husak appointed the first largely non-Communist government in Czechoslovakia since 1948, and resigned. Alexander Dubček was elected speaker of the federal parliament on December 28 and Vaclav Havel the President of Czechoslovakia on December 29, 1989.

In June 1990 Czechoslovakia held its first democratic elections since 1946.

Upheaval in Bulgaria

Main article: End of Communism in Bulgaria (1989)

On November 10, 1989 — the day after the Berlin Wall was breached — Bulgaria's long-serving leader Todor Zhivkov was ousted by his Politburo. Moscow apparently approved the leadership change, despite Zhivkov's reputation as a slavish Soviet ally. Yet, Zhivkov's departure was not enough to satisfy the growing pro-democracy movement. By the time the impact of Mikhail Gorbachev's reform program in the Soviet Union was felt in Bulgaria in the late 1980s, the Communists, like their leader, had grown too feeble to resist the demand for change for long. In November 1989 demonstrations on ecological issues were staged in Sofia, and these soon broadened into a general campaign for political reform. The Communists reacted by deposing the decrepit Zhivkov and replacing him with Petar Mladenov, but this gained them

People on the streets of Sofia (in front of the Parliament) during 1989

only a short respite. In February 1990 the Communist Party, forced by street protests gave up its claim on power and in June 1990 the first free elections since 1931 were held, won by the Bulgarian Socialist Party (the new name of the Communist Party). Although Zhivkov eventually faced trial in 1991, he escaped the violent fate of his northern comrade, → Romanian President → Nicolae Ceauşescu.

The Romanian Revolution

Military and civilians fighting against Ceausescu's regime with the support of a BTR-60 armoured personnel carrier

Main article: → Romanian Revolution of 1989

Unlike other Eastern European countries, Romania had never undergone even limited de-Stalinization. In November 1989, Ceauşescu, then aged 71, was re-elected for another five years as leader of the Romanian Communist Party, signalling that he intended to ride out the anti-Communist uprisings sweeping the rest of Eastern Europe. As Ceauşescu prepared to go on a state visit to Iran, his Securitate ordered the arrest and exile of a local Hungarian-speaking Calvinist minister, Laszlo Tokes, on 16 December, for sermons offending the regime. Tokes was seized, but only after serious rioting erupted. Timişoara was the first city to react, on 16 December, and it remained rioting for 5 days.

Returning from Iran, Ceauşescu ordered a mass rally in his support outside Communist Party headquarters in Bucharest. However, to his shock, the crowd booed as he spoke. After learning about the incidents (both from Timişoara and from Bucharest) from Western radio stations, years of repressed dissatisfaction boiled to the surface throughout the Romanian populace and even among elements in Ceauşescu's own government, and the demonstrations spread throughout the country. At first the security forces obeyed Ceauşescu's orders to shoot protesters, but on the morning of 22 December, the Romanian military suddenly changed sides. Army tanks began moving towards the Central Committee building with crowds swarming alongside them. The rioters forced open the doors of the Central Committee building in an attempt to get Ceauşescu and his wife, Elena, in their grip, but they managed to escape via a helicopter waiting for them on the roof of the building.

Although elation followed the flight of the Ceauşescus, uncertainty surrounded their fate. On Christmas Day, Romanian television showed the Ceauşescus facing a hasty trial, and then suffering summary execution. An interim National Salvation Front Council took over and announced elections for April 1990. The first elections were actually held on May 20, 1990.

Albania

Main article: End of Communism in Albania (1991)

In the Socialist People's Republic of Albania, Enver Hoxha, who ruled Albania for four decades with an iron fist, died 11 April 1985. Eventually the new regime introduced some liberalization, including measures in 1990 providing for freedom to travel abroad. Efforts were begun to improve ties with the outside world. March 1991 elections left the former Communists in power, but a general strike and urban opposition led to the formation of a coalition cabinet including non-Communists. Albania's former Communists were routed in elections March 1992, amid economic collapse and social unrest.

20 February 1991. People in Albania tearing down and demolishing the statue of Enver Hoxha

Yugoslavia

Main article: Breakup of Yugoslavia

In the Socialist Federal Republic of Yugoslavia, the suppression of national identities escalated with the so-called Croatian Spring of 1970-71. After Tito's death in 1980, ethnic tension grew in Yugoslavia. Serbian communist leader Slobodan Miloševic, the new strong man of Yugoslavia, tried to play on the revived Serb nationalism, but ended up alienating all the other ethnic groups in the federation.

End of the Cold War

On December 3, 1989, the leaders of the two world superpowers, U.S. President George H.W. Bush and U.S.S.R. leader Mikhail Gorbachev, declared an end to the Cold War at a summit in Malta. In July 1990, the final obstacle to German reunification was removed when West German Chancellor Helmut Kohl convinced Gorbachev to drop Soviet objections to a reunited Germany within NATO in return for substantial German economic aid to the Soviet Union.

On July 1, 1991, the Warsaw Pact was officially dissolved at a meeting in Prague. At a summit later that same month, Gorbachev and Bush declared a US–Soviet strategic partnership, decisively marking the end of the Cold War. President Bush declared that US–Soviet cooperation during the 1990–91 Gulf War had laid the groundwork for a partnership in resolving bilateral and world problems.

Collapse of the Soviet Union

Main article: History of the Soviet Union (1985-1991)

See also: Singing Revolution, April 9 tragedy, and Jeltoqsan

As the Soviet Union rapidly withdrew its forces from Eastern Europe, the spillover from the 1989 upheavals began reverberating throughout the Soviet Union itself. Agitation for self-determination led to first Lithuania, and then Estonia, Latvia and Armenia declaring independence. Disaffection in other Soviet republics, such as Georgia and Azerbaijan, was countered by promises of greater decentralization. More open elections led to the election of candidates opposed to Communist Party rule.

Glasnost had inadvertently released the long-suppressed national sentiments of all peoples within the borders of the multinational Soviet state. These nationalist movements were further strengthened by the rapid deterioration of the Soviet economy, whereby Moscow's rule became a convenient scapegoat for economic troubles. Gorbachev's reforms had failed to improve the economy, with the old Soviet command structure completely breaking down. One by one, the constituent republics created their own economic systems and voted to subordinate Soviet laws to local laws.

The Baltic Way, reflecting the peak of the Singing Revolution.

In an attempt to halt the rapid changes to the system, a group of Soviet hard-liners represented by Vice-President Gennadi Yanayev launched a coup overthrowing Gorbachev in August 1991. Boris Yeltsin, then president of the Russian SFSR, rallied the people and much of the army against the coup and the effort collapsed. Although restored to power, Gorbachev's authority had been irreparably undermined. In September, the Baltic states were granted independence. On December 1, Ukrainian voters approved independence from the Soviet Union in a referendum. On December 26, 1991, the Soviet Union was officially disbanded, breaking up into fifteen constituent parts, thereby ending the world's largest and most influential Communist state, and leaving China to that position.

Socialism outside Europe

See also: 1990 Democratic Revolution in Mongolia

In the People's Republic of China, the Communist Party of China implemented market reforms before and after collapse of the Eastern Bloc. Similar reform path was taken in the Socialist Republic of Vietnam with Doi Moi. In the People's Republic of Mongolia, the 1990 Democratic Revolution ended the socialist dictatorship. Mengistu Haile Mariam's Soviet-backed dictatorship came to end when he fled Ethiopia in 1991. In Cambodia, Khmer Rouge and Vietnam's puppet regime lost power following UN-sponsored elections in 1993.

What had happened

See also: Predictions of Soviet collapse

The events caught many by surprise. Predictions of the Soviet Union's impending demise had been often dismissed.[9]

Bartlomiej Kaminski's book *The Collapse Of State Socialism* argued that the state socialist system has a lethal paradox: "policy actions designed to improve performance only accelerate its decay".[10]

By the end of 1989, revolts had spread from one capital to another, ousting the regimes imposed on Eastern Europe after World War II. Even the isolationist Stalinist regime in Albania was unable to stem the tide. Gorbachev's abrogation of the Brezhnev Doctrine was perhaps the key factor that enabled the popular uprisings to succeed. Once it became evident that the feared Red Army would not intervene to crush dissent, the Eastern European regimes were exposed as vulnerable in the face of popular uprisings against the one-party system and power of secret police.

Coit D. Blacker wrote in 1990 that the Soviet leadership "appeared to have believed that whatever loss of authority the Soviet Union might suffer in Eastern Europe would be more than offset by a net increase in its influence in western Europe." [11] Nevertheless, it is unlikely that Gorbachev ever intended for the complete dismantling of Communism and the Warsaw Pact. Rather, Gorbachev assumed that the Communist parties of Eastern Europe could be reformed in a similar way to the reforms he hoped to achieve in the CPSU. Just as *perestroika* was aimed at making the Soviet Union more efficient economically and politically, Gorbachev believed that the Comecon and Warsaw Pact could be reformed into more effective entities. However, Alexander Yakovlev, a close advisor to Gorbachev, would later state that it would have been "absurd to keep the system" in Eastern Europe. Yakovlev had come to the conclusion that the Soviet-dominated Comecon could not work on non-market principles and that the Warsaw Pact had "no relevance to real life." [7]

Overcoming legacies of socialism

Further information: Decommunization, Decommunization in Russia, Communist crime, and Communist genocide

Decommunization is a process of overcoming the legacies of the communist state establishments, culture, and psychology in the post-Communist states. Compared with the efforts of the other former constituents of the Soviet bloc and the Soviet Union, decommunization in Russia has been restricted to half-measures, if conducted at all.[12]

Having experienced horrors of socialism, including genocides and atrocities, many nations have taken tough measures against socialism. In several European countries, endorsing or attempting to justify Nazi or Communist genocide will be punishable by up to years of imprisonment.[13]

Commemorations

* German Unity Day in Germany - A national holiday commemorating the anniversary of German reunification in 1990
* Statehood Day in Slovenia - A public holiday commemorating the Slovenia's declaration of independence from Yugoslavia in 1991
* Day of National Unity in Georgia - is a public holiday commemorating victims of the April 9 tragedy
* National Day in Hungary
* Constitution Day in → Romania - Commemorates the 1991 Romanian Constitution that enshrined the return to democracy after the fall of the Communist regime.
* Struggle for Freedom and Democracy Day in the Czech Republic
* Memorials for the Tiananmen Square protests of 1989

This list is incomplete; you can help by expanding it [14].

Symbols and memorials

* Gate Number Two in Poland
* Memorial to the victims of Communism in the Czech Republic
* Lennon Wall in the Czech Republic
* Dawn of Liberty in Kazakhstan - A monument dedicated to Jeltoqsan
* Memorial of Rebirth in Romania

This list is incomplete; you can help by expanding it [14].

See also: KGB victim memorials and Mass graves in the Soviet Union

Museums

- Museum of Communism in Prague, Czech Republic
- House of Terror in Hungary
- Stasi museum in the old headquarters
- Museum of Soviet occupation in Kiev, Ukraine
- Museum of Soviet Occupation in Tbilisi, Georgia
- Museum of the Occupation of Latvia
- Museum of Occupations (Estonia)
- Museum of Occupation (Vilnius)
- Global Museum On Communism, an online museum

This list is incomplete; you can help by expanding it [14].

Books and films

- The Soviet Story - An award-winning documentary film about the Soviet Union.
- The Singing Revolution - A documentary film about the Singing Revolution.
- Heaven on Earth: The Rise and Fall of Socialism - A book and a documentary film based on the book
- Lenin's Tomb: The Last Days of the Soviet Empire - A Pulitzer Prize-awarded book

This list is incomplete; you can help by expanding it [14].

See also

- Color revolutions
- Commonwealth of Independent States

References

This article incorporates information from the revision as of 1 April 2006 of the equivalent article on the Polish Wikipedia.

[1] See various uses of this term in the following publications (http://books.google.com/books?q="Autumn+of+Nations"&btnG=Search+ Books). The term is a play on a more widely used term for 1848 revolutions, the Spring of Nations.

[2] E. Szafarz, "The Legal Framework for Political Cooperation in Europe" in *The Changing Political Structure of Europe: Aspects of International Law*, Martinus Nijhoff Publishers. ISBN 0-7923-1379-8. p.221 (http://books.google.com/books?ie=UTF-8& vid=ISBN0792313798&id=oGGSGhFbCDEC&pg=PA221&lpg=PA221&dq="Autumn+of+Nations"& sig=MNi06rhiCjmU4axaQFavL9u_4Dk).

[3] Sorin Antohi and Vladimir Tismăneanu, "Independence Reborn and the Demons of the Velvet Revolution" in *Between Past and Future: The Revolutions of 1989 and Their Aftermath*, Central European University Press. ISBN 963-9116-71-8. p.85 (http://books.google.com/ books?ie=UTF-8&vid=ISBN9639116718&id=1pl5T45FwIwC&pg=PA85&lpg=PA85&dq="Autumn+of+Nations"& sig=DCpWFx3kS95ahhNIf3omlu5E7sk).

[4] Boyes, Roger (2009-06-04). " World Agenda: 20 years later, Poland can lead eastern Europe once again (http://www.timesonline.co.uk/ tol/news/world/world_agenda/article6430833.ece)". *The Times.* . Retrieved 2009-06-04.

[5] Piotr Sztompka, preface to *Society in Action: the Theory of Social Becoming*, University of Chicago Press. ISBN 0-226-78815-6. p. x (http:// books.google.com/books?ie=UTF-8&vid=ISBN0226788156&id=sdSw3FgVOS4C&pg=PP16&lpg=PP16&dq="Autumn+of+ Nations"&sig=NZAz9ZZ4N0J7wsnpqqrHtL2iG8g).

[6] Romania - Soviet Union and Eastern Europe (http://countrystudies.us/romania/75.htm), *U.S. Library of Congress*

[7] Steele, Jonathan. Eternal Russia: Yeltsin, Gorbachev and the Mirage of Democracy. Boston: Faber, 1994.

[8] Poland:Major Political Reform Agreed (http://www.2facts.com), *Facts on File World News Digest*, 24 March 1989. Facts on File News Services. 6 September 2007

[9] Cummins, Ian (23 December 1995). "The Great MeltDown". The Australian.

[10] The Collapse Of State Socialism (http://www.foreignaffairs.com/articles/47325/robert-legvold/the-collapse-of-state-socialism) Foreign Affairs

[11] Coit D. Blacker. "The Collapse of Soviet Power in Europe." *Foreign Affairs*. 1990.

[12] Karl W. Ryavec. *Russian Bureaucracy: Power and Pathology*, 2003, Rowman & Littlefield, ISBN 0-847-69503-4, page 13

[13] Is Holocaust denial against the law? (http://www.annefrank.org/content.asp?PID=888&LID=2) Anne Frank House

- Dietmar Schultke: Keiner kommt durch - Die Geschichte der innerdeutschen Grenze und der Berliner Mauer, Aufbau-Verlag Berlin 2008
- Levesque, Jacques (1997). *The Enigma of 1989: The USSR and the Liberation of Eastern Europe* (http://ark. cdlib.org/ark:/13030/ft4q2nb3h6/). University of California Press. p. 275. ISBN 978-0520206311. http://ark. cdlib.org/ark:/13030/ft4q2nb3h6/.

External links

- The History of 1989: The Fall of Communism in Eastern Europe (http://chnm.gmu.edu/1989)
- Some of aspects of state national economy evolution in the system of the international economic order. (http://simon31.narod.ru/syndromeofsocialism.htm)

Braşov Rebellion

The **1987 Rebellion of Braşov** was a revolt against → Nicolae Ceauşescu's economic policies in → Communist Romania.

Beginning in late 1986, the seeds of the → Romanian Revolution of 1989 were sown, as workers throughout this Soviet Bloc country mobilized in protest of communist leader Nicolae Ceauşescu's economic policies. Labor uprisings sprouted in the major industrial centers of Cluj-Napoca (November 1986) and Nicolina, Iaşi (February 1987), culminating in a massive strike in Braşov, → Romania's second city. Ceauşescu's "draconian [economic] measures" sought to curb food and energy consumption and reduce

Braşov monument in memory of anti communist fighters, 1944–1989

worker's wages, leading to what Romanian emigre Vladimir Tismăneanu calls an "all pervasive discontent," making Romania "the Eastern Bloc country most vulnerable to revolution." Though Romania was the last of the Eastern European communist strongholds to succumb to → revolution in 1989, his sentiments capture the social and economic volatility of Romania in the late 1980s. The Braşov Revolt reflected this instability; moreover, it was the one of the first large-scale public uprisings against the Ceauşescu regime.

Located in southeastern Transylvania, Braşov was Romania's most industrially developed city, with over 61% of labor participating in industry. A skilled working class emerged in the 1960s as the Communist government forced migrations of Moldavian peasants to operate Braşov factories. Therefore, the industrial decline in Eastern Europe during the mid-1980s hit Braşov and its workers especially hard. Ceauşescu's debt reduction plan beginning in 1982 led to the collapse of the consumer market of the city. (Money intended for food production and distribution was in turn diverted to debt payment to the West.) Therefore, the state rationed key foodstuff and consumer goods, leading to long lines for the most basic commodities. It is in this climate of economic depression and food shortages that the Braşov Rebellion erupted on November 15 1987.

Early on the morning of the 15th, a local elections day, workers at the local Steagul Roşu plant (truck manufacturer) protested reduced salaries and the proposed elimination of 15,000 jobs in the city. Roughly 20,000 workers walked off the job and marched toward the Communist headquarters at the city center. Firstly, the demonstrators expressed loudly wage claims, then they shouted slogans like "Down with Ceauşescu!", "Down with Communism!", chanting anthems of the 1848 Revolution "Down with the Dictatorship" and "We want bread." Over 20,000 workers from the Braşov Tractor Plant, Hidromecanica factory and a number of townspeople joined the march. The combined mob sacked the headquarters building and city hall "throwing into the square portraits of Ceauşescu, and food from the well-stocked canteen." In a time of drastic food shortages, protesters were particularly angered to find festively prepared official buildings and food abundance in order to celebrate the local election victory. A massive bonfire of party records and propaganda burned for hours in the city square. By dusk, Securitate forces and the military surrounded the city center and disbanded the revolt by force. Though no one was killed, some 300 protesters were arrested. However, since the regime decided to play down the uprising as "isolated cases of hooliganism," sentences did not exceed 2 years prison, which was a relatively moderate penalty in the communist penal code. After 1990, up to 100 prison convictions could be documented so far, while others have been forcibly relocated throughout the country.

Though the Braşov Rebellion did not directly lead to revolution, it dealt a serious blow to the Ceauşescu regime, and its confidence in the trade unions. This revolt reflected what historian Denis Deletant refers to as "Ceauşescu's inability to heed the warning signs of increasing labor unrest, plunging blindly forward with the same [economic] measures, seemingly indifferent to their consequences." Therefore, the Braşov Rebellion underscored the growing discontent among workers against the Ceauşescu regime; moreover, it foreshadowed the popular uprisings that would bring down the regime and Communism in Romania. (Rebellion returned to Braşov in December 1989, while Romanians ousted the regime and executed Ceauşescu.)

References

- Deletant, Denis. "Romania, 1948-1989: A Historical Overview" [1], 35-36, *Parallel History Project* on NATO and the Warsaw Pact.
- Keil, Thomas J.. "The State and Labor Conflict in Post-Revolutionary Romania", *Radical History Review*, Issue 82 (Winter 2002), pp. 9-36.
- Kuran, Timur. "Now Out of Never: The Element of Surprise in the East European Revolution of 1989." *World Politics*, Vol. 44, No. 1. (October 1991), pp. 7-48.
- Nelson, Daniel. "The Worker and Political Alienation in Communist Europe", Polity Journal, Vol. 10, No.3, 1978, pp. 1-12.
- Socor, Vladimir. "The Workers' Protest in Braşov: Assessment and Aftermath", Romania Background Report 231, Radio Free Europe Research, 4 December 1987, pp. 3-10.

List of books about the Romanian Revolution of 1989

Books about the → **Romanian Revolution of 1989**.

In Romanian

- ***, *Însemnări din zilele revoluţiei. Decembrie '89*, Bucharest, 1990
- ***, *România 16-22 decembrie. Sînge, durere, speranţă*, Bucharest, 1990
- ***, *Televiziunea Română, Revoluţia română în direct*, Bucharest, 1990
- ***, *Timişoara 16-22 decembrie 1989*, Timişoara, 1990
- ***, *Vom muri şi vom fi liberi*, Bucharest, 1990
- ***, *Revoluţia română văzută de ziarişti americani şi englezi*, Bucharest, 1991
- ***, *O enigmă care împlineşte 7 ani*, Bucharest, 1997
- ***, *E un început în tot sfîrşitul*, Bucharest, 1998
- ***, *Atunci ne-am mântuit de frică* (photo album), Timişoara, 1999
- ***, *Decembrie 89 în presa italiană*, Bucharest 1999
- ***, *Iaşi, 14 decembrie 1989, începutul revoluţiei române?*, Oradea, 2000
- ***, *Întrebări cu şi fără răspuns*, Timişoara, 2001
- Vartan Arachelian, *Revoluţia şi personajele sale*, Bucharest, 1998
- Mihai Babiţchi, *Revoltă în labirint*, Alba Iulia, 1995
- Angela Băcescu, *România '89. Din nou în calea năvălirilor barbare*, Bucharest, 1995
- Veronica Balaj, *Jurnal de Timişoara. 16-22 decembrie 1989*, Timişoara, 1991
- Costel Balint,
  - *1989. Timişoara în decembrie*, Timişoara, 1992
  - *Lumină şi speranţă. Timişoara 1989*, Timişoara, 1994
  - *1989 - Legiunea revoluţiei*, Timişoara, 2005
- Elena Băncilă, *Trage, laşule!*, Bucharest, 1990
- Matei Barbu, *Cap de afiş: Revoluţia de la Timişoara*, Timişoara, 1999
- Mariana Cernicova, *Noi suntem poporul*, Timişoara, 2004
- Ruxandra Cesereanu, *Decembrie '89. Deconstrucţia unei revoluţii*, Iaşi, 2004
- Radu Ciobotea, *După revoluţie, târziu*, Timişoara, 1995
- Ion Coman,
  - *Timişoara. Zece ani de la sîngerosul decembrie 1989*, Bucharest, Sylvi Publishing House, 2000
  - *Omul se duce, faptele rămân, istoria însă le va analiza*, Bucharest, Meditaţii Publishing House, 2007
- Pavel Coruţ, *Să te naşti sub steaua noastră!*, Bucharest, 1993
- Iosif Costinaş, *M-am întors*, Timişoara, 2003
- Teodor Crişan, *Decembrie '89. Revoluţie sau lovitură de palat*, Arad, 2000
- Romulus Cristea,
  - *Revoluţia 1989*, Editura România pur şi simplu, Bucharest 2006
  - *Mărturii de la baricadă*, Editura România pur şi simplu, Bucharest 2007
- Nicolae Danciu-Petniceanu, *Tot ce am pe suflet*, Baia Mare, 1995
- Mihail Decean, *Mărturiile unui naiv corigibil sau Singur printre securişti* [1], Timişoara, 2006
- Viorel Domenico, *Ceauşescu la Târgovişte, 22-25 decembrie 1989*, Bucharest, 1999
- Tit Liviu Domşa, *Împuşcaţi-i, că nu-s oameni!*, Cluj-Napoca, 1998-1999
- Petru Dugulescu, *Ei mi-au programat moartea*, Timişoara, 2003

- Nicolae Durac, *Neliniştea generalilor*, Timişoara, 1990
- Victor Frunză, *Revoluţia împuşcată sau PCR după 22 decembrie 1989*, Bucharest, 1994
- Ion Iliescu,

  - *Revoluţie şi reformă*, Bucharest, 1993; revised edition, 1994
  - *Revoluţia trăită*, Bucharest, 1995
  - *Momente de istorie*, Bucharest, 1995
- Petru Ilieşu, *Timişoara 1989 - No Comment?*, Timişoara, Planetarium, 2004
- Institutul Revoluţiei,

  - *Caietele revoluţiei*, Bucharest, 1/2005 [2]; 2/2005; 1/2006; 2/2006; 3/2006 [3]; 4/2006; 5/2006 [4]; 1/2007 [5]; 2/2007
  - *Clio 1989*, Bucharest 2005
- Cicerone Ioniţoiu, *Album al eroilor decembrie 1989*, Sibiu, 1998
- Sabin Ivan, *Pe urmele adevărului*, Constanţa, 1996
- Eugenia Laszlo, *Timişoara, atunci* [6], Timişoara, 1998
- Dorian Marcu, *Moartea Ceauşeştilor*, Bucharest, 1991
- Dumitru Mazilu, *Revoluţia furată*, Bucharest, 1991
- Florin Medeleţ, *O cronică a revoluţiei din Timişoara 16-22 decembrie 1989*, Timişoara, 1990
- Miodrag Milin,

  - *Timişoara 15-21 decembrie '89*, Timişoara, 1990 part 1 [7], part 2 [8], part 3 [9], part 4 [10]
  - *Timişoara în revoluţie şi după*, Timişoara, 1997
  - *Timişoara în arhivele Europei Libere*, Bucharest, 1999
- Marius Mioc,

  - *Falsificatorii istoriei*, Timişoara 1994; second revised edition, 1995
  - *Revoluţia din Timişoara aşa cum a fost*, Timişoara, 1997
  - *Revoluţia din Timişoara şi falsificatorii istoriei* [11], Timişoara, 1999
  - *Revoluţia, fără mistere. Începutul revoluţiei române: cazul Laszlo Tokes* [12], Timişoara, 2002
  - *Curtea Supremă de Justiţie - Procesele revoluţiei din Timişoara (1989)* [13], Timişoara, 2004
  - *Revoluţia din 1989 şi minciunile din Jurnalul Naţional* [14], Timişoara, 2005
  - *Revoluţia din 1989 pe scurt*, Timişoara, 2006
- Bogdan Murgescu (coordinator), *Revoluţia romănă din 1989. Istorie şi memorie*, Polirom, Iaşi, 2007
- Costel Neacşu, *Religiozitatea revoluţiei romăne din decembrie 1989*, Alba Iulia, 2007
- Sergiu Nicolaescu,

  - *Revoluţia. Începutul adevărului*, Bucharest, 1995
  - *Cartea revoluţiei romăne decembrie '89*, Bucharest, 1999
- Aurel Perva, Carol Roman,

  - *Misterele revoluţiei romăne*, Bucharest, 1990
  - *Misterele revoluţiei romăne - revenire după ani*, Bucharest, 1998
- Ion Pitulescu,

  - *Şase zile care au zguduit România*, Bucharest, 1995
  - *Anul nou se naşte în sânge!*, Bucharest, 1998
- Vasile Popa, *Procesul de la Timişoara*, Timişoara, 1990
- Rodica Popescu, *Miracol? Revoluţie? Lovitură de stat?*, Bucharest, 1990
- Radu Portocală, *România. Autopsia unei lovituri de stat*, Bucharest, 1991
- Dumitru Preda, *1989. Principiul dominoului*, Bucharest, 2000
- Antonina Radoş, *Complotul securităţii. Revoluţia trădată din România*, Bucharest, 1999
- Valentin Raiha, *KGB a aruncat în aer România cu complicitatea unui grup de militari*, Bucharest, 1995

- Nestor Rateş, *România: Revoluţia încâlcită*, Bucharest, 1995
- Şerban Săndulescu, *Decembrie '89. Lovitura de stat a confiscat revoluţie română*, Bucharest, 1996
- Alexandru Saucă, *KGB-ul şi revoluţia română*, Bucharest, 1994
- Constantin Sava, Constantin Monac,

    - *Adevăr despre decembrie 1989*, Bucharest, 1999
    - *Revoluţia română din decembrie 1989 retrăită prin documente şi mărturii*, Bucharest, 2001
- Ioan Scurtu,

    - *Sfîrşitul dictaturii*, Bucharest, 1990
    - *Revoluţia din decembrie 1989 în context internaţional*, Bucharest, 2006
- Cassian Maria Spiridon, *Iaşi 14 decembrie 1989, începutul revoluţiei române*, Iaşi, 1994
- Alex Mihai Stoenescu,

    - *Interviuri despre revoluţie*, Bucharest, 2004
    - *Istoria loviturilor de stat din România*, vol. 4 (I): "Revoluţia din decembrie 1989 - o tragedie românească", Bucharest, 2004
    - *Istoria loviturilor de stat din România*, vol. 4 (II): "Revoluţia din decembrie 1989 - o tragedie românească", Bucharest, 2005
- Ilie Stoian, *Decembrie '89 "criminala capodoperă"*, Bucharest, 1998
- Nicolae Stroescu, *Pe urmele revoluţiei*, Bucharest, 1992
- Titus Suciu,

    - *Reportaj cu sufletul la gură*, Timişoara, 1990
    - *Lumea bună a balconului*, Timişoara, 1995
- Ion Ţârlea, *Moartea pândeşte sub epoleţi. Sibiu '89*, Bucharest, 1993
- Filip Teodorescu, *Un risc asumat*, Bucharest, 1992
- Radu Tinu, *Timişoara... no comment!*, Bucharest, 1999
- Laszlo Tokes, *Asediul Timişoarei*, Oradea, 1999
- Tiberiu Urdăreanu, *1989 - martor şi participant*, Bucharest, 1996

In French

- Radu Portocală, *Autopsie du coup d'Etat roumain*, Calmann-Levy, Paris, 1990 ISBN 2-7021-1935-2

In English

- Sorin Antohi, Vladimir Tismăneanu, *Between Past and Future: The Revolutions of 1989 and Their Aftermath*, Central European University Press, Budapest, 2000
- Ivo Banac (ed.), *Eastern Europe in Revolution*: Katherine Verdery, Gail Klingman, "Romania After Ceausescu: Post-communist Communism", Cornell University Press, Ithaca, 1992 ISBN 0-8014-9997-6
- Andrei Codrescu, *The Hole in the Flag: A Romanian Exile's Story of Return and Revolution*, William Morrow and Co., New York City, 1991 ISBN 0-688-08805-8
- Marius Mioc, *The Anticommunist Romanian Revolution of 1989* [14], Editura Marineasa, Timişoara, 2002; second edition 2004
- Steven D. Roper, *Romania: The Unfinished Revolution*, Routledge, London, 2000 ISBN 9058230279
- Peter Siani-Davies, *The Romanian Revolution of December 1989*, Cornell University Press, Ithaca, 2005 ISBN 0-801-44245-1
- George Galloway and Bob Wylie, *Downfall: The Ceausescus and the Romanian Revolution*, Futura Publications, 1991 ISBN 0-7088-5003-0

Petru Ilieşu, Timişoara 1989 - No Comment?, Timişoara, Planetarium, 2004

In German

* Anneli Ute Gabanyi, *Die unvollendete Revolution: Rumänien zwischen Diktatur und Demokratie*, Piper Verlag, Munich, 1990 ISBN 3492112714

In Hungarian

* Jozsef Gazda, *Megváltó karácsony*, Budapest, 1990
* Laszlo Tokes,
    * *Temesvár ostroma '89*, Budapest, 1990
    * *Temesvári memento*, Oradea, 1999

Multilingual

* Istvan Tolnay, *1989-1999. După zece ani. Tíz év múltán. Ten years after*, Oradea, 1999 (Romanian-Hungarian-English)

See also

* → List of films about the Romanian Revolution of 1989

List of films about the Romanian Revolution of 1989

Films about the → **Romanian Revolution of 1989**.

Fiction

* *Sindromul Timişoara - Manipularea*, 2004, *Sindromul Timişoara - Manipularea* [1] at the Internet Movie Database
* *Cincisprezece*, 2005, *15* [2] at the Internet Movie Database
* *East of Bucharest*, 2006 *A fost sau n-a fost?* [3] at the Internet Movie Database
* *The Paper Will Be Blue*, 2006 *Hîrtia va fi albastră* [4] at the Internet Movie Database
* *The Way I Spent the End of the World*, 2006 *Cum mi-am petrecut sfârşitul lumii* [5] at the Internet Movie Database

Non-fiction

* *A Lesson in Dying*, date unknown
* *A Day in Bucharest*, date unknown
* *Let There Be Peace in this House*, date unknown
* *Requiem für Dominik*, 1990 *Requiem für Dominik* [6] at the Internet Movie Database
* *Dateline: 1989, Romania*, 1991
* *Videogramme einer Revolution*, 1992 *Videogramme einer Revolution* [7] at the Internet Movie Database

See also

- Books about the Romanian Revolution of 1989

References

- *Multinational Documentaries on Eastern Europe*, at the Russian and East European Institute [8] (Indiana University)

Article Sources and Contributors

Romanian Revolution of 1989 *Source*: http://en.wikipedia.org/w/index.php?title=Romanian_Revolution_of_1989 *Contributors*: A2Kafir, ADude, Abi79, AdrianTM, Aetil, Aivazovsky, Alex:D, Alleborgo, Altenmann, Andreidude, Andrwsc, Arado, Arie Inbar, Ashley Pomeroy, Barbatus, Barbesz, Biot, Biruitorul, Blakut, Blue Elf, Bobblehead, Bogdangiusca, Bogdantudor, Bonaparte, Bongwarrior, BorgQueen, Bryan Derksen, Camulod, CapitalElll, Cjthellama, CommonsDelinker, Corneliu-d, Craigy144, Criztu, DJac75, Da Joe, DagosNavy, Dahn, Davecrosby uk, David Edgar, Ddung, Delirium, Denisutku, Desiphral, Dinomite, Donreed, Dorin.lazar, Dpotop, DrFlo1, Dudeman5685, Dwo, ES Vic, Edivorce, El C, Eugeniu B, Everyking, Evlekis, GagHalfrunt, Gagugantu, Gazpacho, Good Olfactory, Gothbag, Grantsky, Greier, Greudin, HanzoHattori, Helmandsare, Hibernian, Hugo999, Hvn0413, Ivan Bajlo, Ivan Bogdanov, IvanLanin, JHCC, Jaraalbe, Jaranda, Jmabel, John, Jokes Free4Me, Jpgordon, Kapitan84, Khoikhoi, Killerman2, KittySaturn, KolyaFrankovich, Krashski35, Leandrod, Lemsjerina, Lightmouse, Lockesdonkey, Marek69, MariusM, MaxSem on AWB wheels, Mazarin07, Mentatus, MiLo28, MihaiC, Mnh123, Naddy, Neilc, Neo-Jay, NerfOne, Nergaal, Nikodemos, Nothingbutmeat, Nv8200p, Oanabay04, One, Orioane, Patrickneil, Pavel Vozenilek, Pearle, PericlesofAthens, Petri Krohn, Pjones27, ProhibitOnions, Quale, RZimmerwald, Radwaddle, Ratza, Rcoving1, Realdevilman, Retired username, Revolutionary, Rezashah4, Rhollenton, Rich Farmbrough, Rjwilmsi, Ronline, Sam Hocevar, Scottmsg, Seabhcan, Sennen goroshi, Sfuerst, ShawnML2, Shii, Sietse Snel, Signalhead, Smallfixer, Sonictruth, Srinivasasha, Stannered, Tabletop, The Anome, The King Of Gondor, TheFEARgod, Tilion, TomH, Tudor hulubei, Turgidson, TypoDotOrg, UDSS, Uk-Kamelot, Underwaterbuffalo, Valentinian, Vashti, Vidor, Vlad, Warfare utf, Wirespot, Woohookitty, XerKibard, Xnuala, Zeisseng, 276 anonymous edits

Romania *Source*: http://en.wikipedia.org/w/index.php?title=Romania *Contributors*: 1111tomica, 334a, A Forgotten Shadow, Aaker, Abi79, Acalamari, Achangeisasgoodasa, Adam78, Adam7davies, Adambiswanger1, Adhalanay, Adhoert, AdiJapan, Adijarca, Adrian two, AdrianCo, AdrianTM, Adrianbg, Adriatikus, Ady4bv, Aesopos, Aeusoes1, Afil, Aflin, Agresivul, Ahoerstemeier, AjaxSmack, Akamad, Akanemoto, Alagemo, Alai, Alastair Rae, Alastairgbrown, Albanman, AlbertR, Aldux, Aledeniz, AlefZet, Alensha, Alex '05, Alex Bakharev, Alex earlier account, Alex:D, Alexander Domanda, Alexandru Busa, AlexiusHoratius, Alexrap, Algos, Alksub, AllyUnion, Altenmann, Amenzix, AmiDaniel, Ana393, Anclation, AndonicO, Andrei George, Andrei Stroe, Andrei nacu, Andrei.badea, Andreidude, Andres, AndrewHowse, Andrewpmk, Andy Marchbanks, Andy8844, Andyjsmith, Andypopa, Angr, Anittas, AnonEMouse, Anonimu, Anonymous Dissident, Antandrus, Antun Gustav, Apancu, Aphaia, AquinasProtocol, Aranherunar, Arcillaroja, Aris Katsaris, Arjun01, ArmadilloFromHell, Armydepot, Arpingstone, ArsalanKhan, Art LaPella, Arthur naghi, Arwel Parry, Asdffdsaqwerty, Asdfghjklasdfjk, Astral, AstroNomer, Aude, Ausseagull, Avala, Avidbrowser, AxG, Ayceman, BD2412, BaNaTeaN, BalkanFever, Baristarim, Baritchi, Barneyboo, Baronnet, Barryob, Basescu, Bash, Basketball110, Baxter9, Bazzajf, Bbenjoe, Beetstra, Bejiita, Beland, Belligero, Bellow, Bencherlite, Beyond silence, Biruitorul, Bizso, Bkell, Black N Red, Black-Velvet, Blaga, Blastwizard, Blue Elf, Bluemask, Bobo192, Bobu1981, Bogdan Stanciu, Bogdan Stancu, Bogdangiusca, Bogdans, Bogmih, Bombonel, Bonaparte, Boothy443, Borat98, BorgHunter, Boshinoi, Boxero, BoyGuy26, Bprmacrae, Branddobbe, Brat32, Breno, Brian, Brianga, Brion VIBBER, BryanHolland, Bryanc 16, Bryndza, Btiganov, Bubupicard, Bucketsofg, Bursck, BusyB, Butseriouslyfolks, CJLL Wright, CLW, CWii, Cabra, Cafzal, Caiaffa, Califate123!, CambridgeBayWeather, Can't sleep, clown will eat me, CanOfWorms, Caniago, Cantus, Caponer, Capricorn42, Carmen22, Carpaticus, Casliber, Catalin Costache, Catasomfy, Cdaylin, Cdc, Ceaunel, Celebration1981, Cenarium, Cglassey, ChKa, Charleca, Chochopk, Chris the speller, ChrisO, Chrism, ChristmasCpp, CieloEstrellado, Cireshoe, Cisum.ili.dilm, City sixty-five, Clay allison, Clerks, Cobie33, Codex Sinaiticus, Codruttg, Colonies Chris, ComUSSR, CommonsDelinker, Compu34, Connorb1992, Constantzeanu, ContributorX, Conversion script, Cool Blue, Cordless Larry, Cosmote, Cosy18, Cotton remote, Count de Ville, Crazy Boris with a red beard, Crazydog8himself, Crazytales, Credema, Crissim99, Cristi.falcas, CristianChirita, Cristibur, Criztu, Crownjewel82, Crystallina, Cucerzan, Curps, Cutzulica27, Cuvtixo, Cwilli201, D12south, D39, D6, DJ1AM, DMacks, DSuser, DVD R W, DW, Dae Jang Geum, Dahn, Dakart, Dalf, Damas, Damian Radu, Damis, DanMS, Daniel Mahu, Daniel Tellman, Daniel5127, Daniel77o, Danielgrad, Danielsavoiu, Dankat24, Danny, Dannym 486, Dansab, Danutz, Davenbelle, David Johnson, David Kernow, David Liuzzo, David R. Ingham, David Sneek, Davidweman, Dc76, De koelie, DeadEyeArrow, Deckchair, Defrenrokorit, Delgadoloayza, Delirium, Delldot, Den fjättrade ankan, DerHexer, Dereye, Deus Ex, Dexileos, Diana Teodorescu, Diego pmc, Discospinster, DivineIntervention, Dleisawitz, Dmaftei, DoctorW, Docu, Domino theory, Domitius, Donald Albury, Dpotop, Dpv, Dpwkbw, Dr.alf, Dracken, Dragosped, Drbug, Drini, Dukeofomnium, Duncan1892, Durexromania, Dysepsion, Dysprosia, E Pluribus Anthony, ES Vic, EU 01, Eachwiped, Eagleridge, East718, Eclecticology, Ed Fitzgerald, EdJohnston, Edchoi, Edgesusedarea, Editorofthewiki, Edivorce, Ehn, El C, Electionworld, Eliade, Elsi mate, Emote, Enciclopedia, EncycloPetey, Epbr123, Epfnc, EronMain, Esperant, Essam101, Essjay, Et lux perpetua luceat eis, Ethnologue Philologue, Etn3580, Eu.stefan, Eumc, Eurocopter, Europeanul, Euthymios, EvanProdromou, Evercat, Everyking, Evil Monkey, EvilAlex, Evlekis, Ex Pluribus Unum, Executor Tassadar, Ezcreator22, Ezeu, F36unp, Fabartus, Fabhcun, Famasownznewbiezz, Fang Aili, Fedallah, Felixpetrar, FeodorBezuhov, Ferkelparade, Fiden, Fillosaurus, Finngall, Firetrap9254, Fisel, Flatterworld, Flav.drag., Fleurstigter, Florin Andrei, Fluffery, Forseti, Fotoprint, Fratrep, FreplySpang, Fsol, FunkyFly, Funnybunny, Future Perfect at Sunrise, G. Campbell, GDP, Gabbe, Gabitzu, Gagugantu, Gaius Cornelius, Galoubet, Garden, Garry Saint, Esquire, Gcbirzan, Gearoid007, Gene Nygaard, Geolyus, Georgia guy, Gggh, Ghenaia, Gheorghef, Ghewgill, Ghita, Giggy, Gilgamesh, Gilliam, Giving is good, as long as you're getting, Glen, Glenn, Gligan, Gogo Dodo, Golbez, Good Olfactory, Goodoldpolonius2, GordyB, GorillazFanAdam, GraemeL, Graham87, Grahamec, Gramaic, Grandmasterka, Green Giant, Green32, GreenSprite, Greier, Grendelkhan, Grimlund, GringoCroco, Grubber, Gsherry, Gurch, Gutza, Gyula19, Gzornenplatz, Hadal, Hadžija, HarpH, Harry Dawes, Hassion, Hawkos, Hebel, HeikoEvermann, Heimstern, Hele 7, HenryLi, Henryhartley, Hexagon1, Hhst, Highpriority, HisSpaceResearch, Hjncfkdnmhbjk, Hmains, Hojimachong, HolyShiznik, Hst20, Husky, Husond, Hvn0413, Hxseek, I already forgot, IJA, Iadrian yu, Iasi, Ibarrutidarruti, Icairns, Icar, Ief, Ihuxley, Illythr, Imalegend, Imomarket, ImperatorExercitus, Indexxs, Infinoid, Infrogmation, Inter, Inter16, Interlingual, Intersofia, IoanOstas, Ioana86, Ioannes Tzimiskes, Iridescent, Irishguy, Irpen, Items cases, Iugin, Iulianu, Ixfd64, Izzedine, J Milburn, J.Wright, J04n, JLogan, JM Robert, JULIA RADESCU IS A SKIVER!, James086, JamesR, Jankaspar, Janneman, Jayjg, Jb0000000000, JdeJ, Jeff3000, Jelloyeti, Jensboot, Jeronimo, JetLover, Jiang, JidGom, JimR, Jimfbleak, Jimmy Slade, Jjmihai, Jmabel, Jni, JoJan, JoSePh, JoanneB, Joelr31, Johann Wolfgang, John, John Carter, Johnleemk, Johny Richards, Jokes Free4Me, Jon Harald Søby, JonHarder, Jonel, Jorunn, Jose77, Joseph Solis in Australia, JoshEdgar, Jossi, Joy, Jredmond, Juganot, Jumbuck, Justin 42069420, Jvmills, KIDB, KJohansson, KaRaKteR, Kafziel, Kaihsu, Kamenaua, Karol Langner, Kassabov, KathrynLybarger, Katieh5584, Kaz, Keelm, Kendrick7, Keoke, Kessler, Kf4bdy, Khoikhoi, Kilhan, Kingturtle, Kintetsubuffalo, Kirill Lokshin, KissL, Kitch, Knepflerle, Knowledge Seeker, KnowledgeOfSelf, Ko2008, Koavf, Konstantin, Korean alpha for knowledge, Kosebamse, Kotiwalo, Koyaanis Qatsi, Kozuch, Kralizec!, Krellis, Krithin, Krylonblue83, Kungfuadam, Kuru, Kuruc, Kutrigur, Kwamikagami, Kwiki, Ky Music Nerd, Kyo2590, L95slovenia, LAX, LOTkid, Lacrimosus, Latinitas, Laubz83, Lazaraf78, Lazio gio, Lcarscad, Le savoir et le savoir-faire, Lear 21, Lekse, Lennonist, Leujohn, Lightdarkness, Lightmouse, Lilac Soul, Ling.Nut, Lionzz, LittleOldMe, Lklundin, Lockesdonkey, Lonelymother2, Looxix, Lucasalvarez, Lucasbfr, Luciandrei, Lucy-marie, Luk, Luke w, Lumos3, MBisanz, MJCdetroit, MJM74, Madalinfocsa, Madenham, Magasin, Maijinsan, Malhonen, Man vyi, Man with one red shoe, Mana Excalibur, Mani1, Manuel007, Maralia, Margana, Mario1987, MariusM, MariusPetruStanica, MariusVasilescu, Mark Ryan, MarkSutton, MarkSweep, MarkVolundNYC, Marksed, Martewa, Martinp23, Martinwilke1980, Marvao, Mashu, Master Jay, Mastermindsro, Mathae, Matthew hk, Mattisbetterthengod, Mauriziotani, Maverick16, Mayuma, Mb nl, McDogm, Meelahds, Melsaran, Mentatus, Messy Baby, Mets501, Mic, Michael Adrian, Michael Devore, Michael Hardy, Mickey gfss2007, Miclovan, Mihai, Mihai Andrei, Mihai Stan, Mihai1025, MihaiC, Mihail ioniu, Mike Rosoft, Mikecron, Mikmik2323, Mild Bill Hiccup, Mimihitam, Minim.ro, Misiu mp, Misza13, Mkosmul, Mmarci, Mocu, Modulatum, Molly Wei, Moncrief, Monikad, Monobook maker, Monor, Moosh88, MoraSique, Motion of Lotion, Moyogo, Mrg3105, Mrnordsee, MykReeve, Mytildebang, Mywayyy, NIR-Warrior, Naddy, Nagytibi, Narrasawa, Naryathegreat, Nat, NawlinWiki, Neiko, Nergaal, Netoholic, Neurolysis, Neutrality, Nighthawk rocks, Nightstallion, NikoSilver, Nikodemos, Nishkid64, Nivix, Nmpenguin, Noah Salzman, Noisettes, Nom DeGuerre, Nomad Terv, NorbertArthur, Northern Romania, Notheruser, NothingMuch, NuclearWarfare, Numbo3, Nv8200p, Nzpcmad, Nerostrateur, NazismIsntCool, O mores, Oatmeal batman, Ocee, Octane, Ohnoitsjamie, Olahus, Olathe, OldakQuill, Olessi, Omicronpersei8, On Thermonuclear War, Open understanding, OpenToppedBus, Orioane, Oscarthecat, Ossmann, Ouishoebean, Out slide, Outesticide, Ovidiu2all, Oxymoron83, P3Pp3r, PANONIAN, PET, Pabix, Page Up, Pagrashtak, Panel 2008, Panex, Panwan, Passaddhi, PaulFCB1899, Paulinho28, Paweł ze Szczecina, PaxEquilibrium, Pbozdog, Pedro, PeeJay2K3, Peeperman, Peer-LAN, Pernambuco, Petan, Petcu.bogdan, PeteVerdon, Peter gk, PeterisP, Petre Buzdugan, Petreg, Phil Boswell, Philip Trueman, Physchim62, Piccolo Modificatore Laborioso, Pichu1988, Piledhigheranddeeper, Pirlinho, Pixi, Playclever, Pmanderson, Poetaris, Pohta ce-am pohtit, Pokrajac, Polaron, Politis, Polyhister, Polylerus, Porcher, Ppetru, Priceangle, Primarycontrol, Prince William on Wheels, Prolog, Pryde 01, Pschemp, Pudeo, Purpleturple, Putinputinputinpoutine, Qaphsiel, QatBurglar, Quadell, Quizimodo (usurped), Qxz, Qyd, RBrancusi, RG2, RHB, RVLTNR, Rab V, RadioKirk, Radualexandru99, Raduwantsyoudead, Radwaddle, Rafa28 alq, Ragnarberg, Ralfy, Ran, RandomP, Rarelibra, Raser63, RattusMaximus, Raven4x4x, Razvanus, Rbifan, Rcristi, Rd232, Rdsmith4, Red Winged Duck, Redgolpe, Redwolf24, Reedy, Rej4sl, Remigiu, Res Gestæ Divi Augusti, Rettetast, Revolutionary, RexNL, Reywas92, Rezistenta, Rhadoo32, Rich Farmbrough, RichAromas, Rick Block, RickK, Rickpedia, Ricky81682, Ridernyc, Rizalninoynapoleon, Rjwilmsi, Ro mlc, Roadrunner11, Roamataa, Rob Salzman, Rob.derosa, Roberta F., Roke, Roksanna, Rolk7, Rom gym, Romania, RomaniaIsntCool, Romaniac, Romanian2, Romanianmonasteries, Romanm, Romano-Dacis, Romanul, Romihaitza, Român, Ronline, Roothee, Rory096, Roxi2, RoyBoy, Roydosan, Rronline, Rubobostes, Ryan4314, S71elements, SEIG HEIL!, SElefant, SU Linguist, Sagaciousuk, SalJyDieBoereKomLei, Salt Yeung, Sam Hocevar, Sam Korn, Sam Vimes, Samantha555, Sambure, Samrolken, Samuel Pepys, Sandstein, Sango123, Santiparam, Sapphic, Saydavid, Saywhat1, Sch. David, Schmeitgeist, Schopenhauer, Scipius, Scooter20, Scott Gall, Screensaver, Secfan, SeekingOne, Sentineneve, SergioGeorgini, Serkanbulan, Sfahey, Shanel, Shanes, Sharkie, Sharksandwich999, Shenme, Sherool, Shimgray, Shoaler, Shoeofdeath, Shoessss, SidP, Sigquit, Silverxxx, Silvescu, Simetrical, SimonD, SimonP, Sir Lothar, Sjacinth, Sjakkalle, Slicing, Smartech, Smashville, SmileToday, Smith2006, Snipa, Snowolf, SoLando, SomeHuman, Sonykus, Sorin Negulescu, Sorincalex, SpNeo, Spangineer, Spellcast, Spellmaster, Spiridon MANOLIU, SpookyMulder, Sqniod, Ssmith619, Ssolbergj, Staxringold, Stebbins, Stefanz 7, Stemonitis, Stephenb, Stevenmitchell, Steventity, Strainu, Strolls, Stupanico, Stwalkerster, Styrofoam1994, Sunray, Supaplexys, Superbeecat, Susvolans, Swarve, Swordsman3003, T2k, TAXIcon, TMLutas, TSO1D, Tabletop, Talensis, Tankard, Tapir Terrific, Tasmaniacs, TastyPoutine, Tavilis, Tawker, Taxman, Tbjablin, Tekken50, Teledu, Telex, Template namespace initialisation script, Terence, Texteditor, The Decay of Meaning, The Evil Spartan, The Obento Musubi, The Ogre, The Palatine, The Phoenix, The Transhumanist, The wub, TheDJ, TheGiantVermin, TheUsedMCRluver13, Theathenae, Thebogusman, Thehelpfulone, Theramblingscot, Therequiembellishere, Theternity, Thiseye, Thu, Thunderboltz, Tidying Up, Tim Starling, TimBentley, Time For Honesty, Timir2, Timor Stultorum, Tjnewell, Tobby72, TodorBozhinov, Tom Peters, Tom-, Tone, Tony1, Tonywalton, Toomontrangle, Tordail, Torzsmokus, Tpbradbury, Travelbird, Trevor MacInnis, Trialsanderrors, Trwesley, Turgidson, Twiz389, Tyler Nash, Typoty, U.S.A.U.S.A.U.S.A., UBeR, Ugen64, Uncle G, Ungvichian, Unknown Unknowns, Unsc, Upsidown, Uris, Ursul pacalit de vulpe, Usergreatpower, Utcursch, Uzo20, V. Szabolcs, Vacekha, Valentinian, Vardion, Vary, Vasile, Veduny, Venatoreng, Victor12, Vintila Barbu, Violetriga, Vlachul, VmoSW, Voice of All, Vpundir, Vsion, Wanderingstan, Wangi, Wayward, WegianWarrior, Welovefred, Welsh, Whimemsz, Whistle25, WhoTheBlank?, Wik, Wiki alf, Wimt, WojPob, Wolfling, Woohookitty, Wwe80, Xanthar, Xasha, Xnacional, Xrtnldys, Xxphil, Yamamoto Ichiro, Yanche, Yanksox, Yodo, Yonas29, Yonatan, Yvesnimmo, ZAn Ton, Zachorious, Zello, Zero Gravitas, Zigger, Zlerman, Zocky, Zoney, Zooleika, Zsombor, Cele Kula, ΚΕΚΡΩΨ, 2482 anonymous edits

Communist Romania *Source*: http://en.wikipedia.org/w/index.php?title=Communist_Romania *Contributors*: A CT Romania, Adhalanay, AdrianTM, Adriatikus, Ahoerstemeier, Al1976, AlbertR, Alex:D, Altenmann, Andrei Stroe, Anonimu, Anonimu din Constanta, Anthony Appleyard, BarbuMare, Barryob, Biruitorul, Bobblewik, Bogdangiusca, CRakovsky, CactusWriter,

Cbrajon, ComUSSR, Conte di Cavour, Criztu, Cybercobra, D39, DIREKTOR, DJ Silverfish, Dahn, Daizus, Danny9510, Dc76, Dcheng, Dekimasu, Domino theory, Dpotop, ES Vic, EdwinHJ, Error, Eugen Ivan, Eugeniu B, EventHorizon09, Everyking, Fabiform, Fixman, Formeruser-81, Forseti 7, Fsol, GCarty, Gaius Cornelius, Gene Nygaard, Georodin, Good Olfactory, Gr8opinionater, Greier, Ground Zero, Grunners, Gurch, Gutza, Hede2000, Iammargi, Ice Cold Beer, Ikarad, Iulianu, Jason M, Jiang, Jmabel, Joseph Solis in Australia, Kamenaua, Lightmouse, Louis88, Lulo.it, Lycurgus, MEJ119, Mannerheim, MathFacts, Mentatus, MihaiC, Mnmazur, Mocu, Mosedschurte, Mario, Naddy, Neilc, Nergaal, OOODDD, OwenBlacker, Pearle, Pharos, Piccadilly Sirkus, Plumpy1995, Pmanderson, Quiensabe, R-41, Remigiu, Rezashah4, Riana, Richwales, RobinCarmody, Romanm, Sceptre, SchuminWeb, Sergiu.dumitriu, SimonP, Smarkflea, Smsarmad, Spellcast, Styrofoam1994, Template namespace initialisation script, Tilion, Timbouctou, Turgidson, Vancouverguy, Vegetator, Vgranucci, Vintila Barbu, Wars, Wik, WikiLaurent, William Avery, Wmahan, Xanthar, Xiner, Zeppy1968, Zocky, Zserghei, 101 anonymous edits

Nicolae Ceauşescu Source: http://en.wikipedia.org/w/index.php?title=Nicolae_Ceau%C5%9Fescu Contributors: 172, Aaronbrick, AdiJapan, Adriatikus, Againme, Agurza, Ahoerstemeier, Ahsere, Aivazovsky, Alai, Albanman, AlbertR, Alex:D, Alexbl02072, Alexrap, Ali@gwc.org.uk, Alma Pater, Altenmann, Amchow78, Anamexis, Andre Engels, Andrei Rublev, Andrei Stroe, Andrew Dalby, Anittas, AnnaFrance, Anonimu, Anonymous from the 21st century, Anonymous from the 21th century, Apancu, Arbeit Sockenpuppe, ArekExcelsior, Arkalochori, Ashley Pomeroy, Attilios, Auno3, Ave Caesar, Azdfg, BYF, Badmachine, Bci2, Bentley4, Berkeley0000, Betacommand, BigHaz, Billcito, Biruitorul, BloomIreland, Bloovee, Bobblewik, Bogdan Stanciu, Bogdangiusca, Bonnifac, Brion VIBBER, Bronks, Buickid, CHJL, CSWarren, Cafzal, Calvin Ho Jiang Lim, Camil, Camptown, Can't sleep, clown will eat me, Cantus, Casinote, CenozoicEra, Cgingold, ChaTo, Cheran, Chrisvls, CielProfond, Clicketyclack, Comrade Tassadar, Connormah, Craigy144, Craxton, Cre119, Crebbin, Criztu, D6, DO'Neil, Dahn, Danielsavoiu, Danny, Dantadd, Darth Panda, DeAceShooter, Dekimasu, Delirium, Delpino, Denisutku, Desiphral, Dezidor, Dgies, DiabloSanchez, Diehardredsoxfan3, Digwuren, Discospinster, Dowew, Dpotop, DrDaveHPP, DrFlo1, DrSamba, Dudeman5685, DynamoJax, EamonnPKeane, EchetusXe, Edcolins, Edward, Ejercito Rojo 1950, Ekki01, El C, Elentirmo, Elizard16, Ellywa, Emykcul, Eran, Error, Everyking, Ezeu, Ferg2k, Fgurtler, Fibonacci, Florinl, Formeruser-81, Formeruser-82, Freakmighty, Fred82, Fvw, GCarty, Gabriel2008, Gabrielro, Gagugantu, Gaius Cornelius, Gammatigerx, Gazpacho, Gcbirzan, Geausescu, Gene Nygaard, Geoffrey Matthews, Gerhard, Gilgamesh, Good Olfactory, Grin, Gromlakh, Ground Zero, Gruen, Guitarpah, Gurch, Guycarmeli, H-Scorpio, HADRIANVS, HFGR, Hadal, Hailey C. Shannon, Haukurth, Hbdragon88, Hede2000, Hellopantsman, Henchio, Hero sparta Gold, Herostratus, Hmains, Hurricane111, Hegesippe Cormier, INkubusse, Icar, Igorf, Ilse@, Infrogmation, InthePast, Iulianu, J.J., JIP, Jackiespeel, Jaranda, Jeff3000, JennaSuzanne, Jeronimo, Jiang, Jimbo Wales, Jmabel, JnB987, JoanneB, John, John Kenney, Joseph Solis in Australia, Josephabradshaw, Joshmaul, Joy, Junes, Jusjih, Just Another Fat Guy, K. Lastochka, Kane5187, Kansas Bear, Karl Meier, Kbdank71, Kchishol1970, Khoikhoi, Killiondude, Kingal86, Kiteinthewind, Kittybrewster, Klackalica, Konstantin, Kpjas, Kransky, Kridily, Kthejoker, Kwamikagami, LOL, Lajos25, Lars69, Lawsonrob, Lemsjerina, Lightmouse, Link2joon, Little guru, Livajo, Loyalist Cannons, Lulugiu, Madhava 1947, Maracana, Mark83, Marsek, MastCell, Masterofzen, Matdrodes, Matthew, Member, Mentatus, Miacek, Mic, Miguel, Milan2t, Mindstar, MinnesotanConfederacy, Mirgheca, Mirv, MisterBee1966, Misterkillboy, Mnmazur, Montrealais, Mountolive, Moviestarr, Mr. Diegos, Mrdie, Mtaylor848, Naddy, Neilc, NellieBly, Nevilley, Nextstep ro, Nick Tinbum, Nickpdx, Nikodemos, Nixdorf, Nk, Nogu, Nv8200p, Oanabay04, OettingerCroat, Ojigiri, Olahus, Olivier, OnBeyondZebrax, OrangeDog, Orzetto, OwenBlacker, Pat1792A, Patrickneil, Patxi lurra, Paulinho28, Phatcat68, Pigsonthewing, Pixel :-), Planetneutral, Polylerus, ProhibitOnions, Pwt898, Ral315, Ralhazzaa, RashersTierney, Rata, Ratza, Raul654, Rdsmith4, Reo11, ReidrM, Revolutionary, RexNL, Rezashah4, Rich Farmbrough, Richard Keatinge, Richwales, Rimush, Rms125a@hotmail.com, RodC, Romanm, Ronline, Ruy Lopez, Salamander03, Sam Hocevar, Sam Spade, Sannse, Santa Sangre, Savedhead1, Sceptre, Schachar, Secretlondon, Sesel, Setchcr, Shu, Silverhorse, Sk0kkekas, Skm2001, SkyWalker, Smack, Smith2006, SouthernComfort, SpiderJon, SpookyMulder, Spot87, Stefan Udrea, Stefanomione, Struway, SummerWithMorons, Supreme Bananas, Swerdnaneb, Szjanos, TMLutas, TOO, Tec15, Tedernst, Telso, The Anome, The Giant Puffin, TheDJ, TheDoober, TheGerm, TheMadBaron, Thewolf37, Thuresson, Tiberiu123, Timothy678, Timothy687, Toba1, Tom the Goober, Tommyt, TravelingDude, Ttk371, Turgidson, Tzigan, Ugen64, Unschool, Valentinian, Van helsing, Vanhoabui, Vanka5, Varlaam, Vdobrea, Vick brown, Vintila Barbu, Virgil Vaduva, Vkem, Vlad, VoX, Wgiuliano, Whimemsz, WhisperToMe, Wiki alf, Willking1979, Woohookitty, Wwilly, Xanthar, XerKibard, Xichael, Xnuala, YUL89YYZ, Yomama14, Ziga, Zocky, Zvar, Zzyzx11, 飛び 女, 606 anonymous edits

History of Romania since 1989 Source: http://en.wikipedia.org/w/index.php?title=History_of_Romania_since_1989 Contributors: A2Kafir, Ahoerstemeier, Altenmann, Anonimu, Biruitorul, Bogdangiusca, Branislavk, Bryan Derksen, Criztu, Daniel1918, Dc76, Donarreiskoffer, DrFlo1, ES Vic, Edcolins, Edebundity, Eugen Ivan, Evercat, Everyking, Fsol, Gcbirzan, Greier, Ground Zero, Herostratus, Jiang, Jmabel, Joseph Solis in Australia, Jschwa1, Judged, Julo, Naddy, Nergaal, Opelio, Paweł ze Szczecina, Pearle, Remigiu, Ricky81682, Rsocol, Simon d, Template namespace initialisation script, Tiddly Tom, Turgidson, Van helsing, 27 anonymous edits

Revolutions of 1989 Source: http://en.wikipedia.org/w/index.php?title=Revolutions_of_1989 Contributors: Admrboltz, AdultSwim, Aivazovsky, Alexander Domanda, Altenmann, Andrwsc, Anittas, Aris 8564, Asmaybe, B.d.mills, Balloonguy, Barabum, Bastiaquinas, Biala Gwiazda, BilCat, BillFlis, Biruitorul, Buffer v2, CO, CanadianLinuxUser, Cdamama, Champlain and St. Lawrence Railroad, ChildofMidnight, Chris the speller, Circeus, CommonsDelinker, Conscious, Daaf, Dale Arnett, Damczyk, DarwinPeacock, Dca5347, DeirYassin, Descendall, Devatipan, Digwuren, Dragostanasie, Dudeman5685, Ejdzej, Elizard16, Eluchil404, Epbr123, Everyking, Ex ottoyuhr, Fdedio, ForestDim, GCarty, Gazpacho, Geoffrey Pruitt, Gestapos, Gf1961, Grantsky, H2ppyme, Hairy Dude, Hires an editor, Hmains, JCDenton2052, Jacurek, Jaraalbe, Jersyko, Jmabel, Joseph Solis in Australia, Juantag, Jusjih, Juyukichi, Kafziel, Kelvinc, Kintetsubuffalo, Kusma, Lacrimosus, Lamato, Lambdoid, Laveol, Lightmouse, Lockesdonkey, Logologist, Matthead, MegX, Merovingian, Mimzy1990, Miranche, Mnh123, Month, Mosedschurte, Nemeng, Nick Moss, Nv8200p, Nwe, OwenBlacker, Pavel Vozenilek, Pazsit Ulla, Pearle, Petri Krohn, Pgan002, Piotrus, Poetaris, Quantumobserver, RZimmerwald, Renata3, Renegade xwo, Rjwilmsi, Robin klein, Samsara, Sharkb, ShoWPiece, Sm8900, Stephenchou0722, SteveMcCluskey, Styrofoam1994, TVCGuy, Tec15, Tempodivalse, Themartinrobinsons, Trevor MacInnis, Tripod86, Tsiaojian lee, Turgidson, Van helsing, Vasi, Verycharpie, Viator slovenicus, Vidor, Viking880, Vints, Warofdreams, Wassermann, Woohookitty, Xeeron, XerKibard, Y, Yaan, Yourroads, 290 anonymous edits

Braşov Rebellion Source: http://en.wikipedia.org/w/index.php?title=Bra%C5%9Fov_Rebellion Contributors: Arie Inbar, Avalon, Biruitorul, Bogdangiusca, Chc2010, Confuzion, Dahn, Digitalux, Himself rock, Hugo999, Meleze, Neddyseagoon, Rich Farmbrough, Roamataa, Tim!, Turgidson, UW, Vintila Barbu, 3 anonymous edits

List of books about the Romanian Revolution of 1989 Source: http://en.wikipedia.org/w/index.php?title=List_of_books_about_the_Romanian_Revolution_of_1989 Contributors: Anclation, Corneliu-d, Dahn, Elonka, Fram, GregorB, MariusM, Paul A, Stefanomione, Turgidson, 19 anonymous edits

List of films about the Romanian Revolution of 1989 Source: http://en.wikipedia.org/w/index.php?title=List_of_films_about_the_Romanian_Revolution_of_1989 Contributors: Bogdangiusca, Bulldog123, Dahn, Kappa, MariusM, Masaruemoto, Stefanomione, Turgidson, Varlaam, 2 anonymous edits

Image Sources, Licenses and Contributors

Lightning Source UK Ltd.
Milton Keynes UK
05 May 2010

153791UK00001B/121/P